–In associat.

Contents

Foreword

As a young child, I had dreamed of owning a dog. My parents also longed for a canine companion, but my allergies made this impossible, and I, as they had, became resigned to a life without one. Even *Boasun*, the family boa constrictor snake, and a tank of tropical fish couldn't satisfy that longing for a pet of the faithful, four-legged kind.

At the ripe old age of sixteen, I began dating a local girl whose parents owned a large, long haired German Shepherd. After finally being invited home to meet them, I left with swollen eyes whilst wheezing and sneezing, desperately sucking on an inhaler to catch my breath. At sixteen, the thought of not being able to breathe and looking like a gargoyle came secondary to having a girlfriend and so I continued to go visit the house despite my allergic reactions.

Over the next six months or so, I discovered that my allergies to her dog became less with every visit and, to my amazement, I came to realise that the more often I was exposed to the dog, the less severe the allergic reactions became.

 The more tolerant I became, the more time I spent with her, and it wasn't long before I was invited on the weekly family dog walk. I use the word 'walk' loosely because what happened was an hour's stroll followed by many foiled attempts to trap the dog to get her back on the lead. Eventually, achieved by a pincer movement any army general would be proud of, we would catch the dog and reattach the lead. This would be closely followed by my girlfriend's father reprimanding the bewildered dog for not coming back.

We would take the dog out most evenings under strict instruction to never let her off lead. However, her parents hadn't considered the fact that we were sixteen years old! How often do you recall doing as your parents told you to at that age? Every night we would let her off the lead and every night she returned when we called her. This presented me with something of a dilemma; I was desperate to tell my girlfriend's dad that replacing smacks and stern reprimands with lots of fuss, praise and treats on the dog's recall would result in his dog returning on cue, rather than being too scared to come back.

To me, it was so obvious that once the dog knew she would get rewarded for her compliance, she would be far more likely to comply. Conversely, being chastised verbally and physically upon each return would cause fear and a reluctance to come back.

Eventually, our juvenile romance ran its course, however it had taught me much about life, both human and canine! Although I didn't realise it at the time, I had happened upon the foundation stones of modern dog training, a practice which is based only on positive reinforcement. This is far more effective than using negative reinforcement (or positive punishment for bad behaviours). This I have found to be true when dealing with humans as well as dogs. It is far easier to teach both dogs and humans the wanted behaviours than to attempt to stop the unwanted ones. The other valuable lesson was that I could overcome my allergies and so it did not take much persuading for my parents to take on Zac, a Doberman pup. A great dog and a wonderful breed, full of life, intelligence and mischief.

My father took Zac to Doberman training, having been led to understand that it had to be breed specific training because Dobermans were said at the time to be hard to train, require a firm hand and specifically require dominance-based training. Knowing what I know now, this was absolute poppycock and it didn't take me long to realise this. My father took Zac every week religiously, but without much progress and Zac never passed out of the beginners' class. My father stopped taking him after the embarrassment of tripping over with all the titbits falling out of his pocket, causing all the dogs from the advanced class that were off the lead to rush over and enjoy the free feast. Once all the handlers had their dogs back under their control, the trainer took great pleasure in belittling my father for, as he put it, 'cheating'. Yet again, it seemed obvious to me that if treats were what inspired the dog to follow a cue or command then using them had to be a better way to teach the dog than bullying it or using force.

Over the next few months, I took great pleasure in taking Zac to the park where the Doberman training took place and standing just outside the training circle. Together, we made a great spectacle as we showcased his obedience, performing an array of tricks using the very methods that the trainer had called 'cheating'. Zac was way ahead of any dog in the advanced class despite him being less than twelve months old. This was my first experience of training a dog; it inspired me to learn more and I developed a thirst for knowledge on all things canine, particularly the behavioural aspects.

Fast forward several years and after owning several dogs, in particular George, a cross breed who is sadly no longer with us, I inevitably became involved in helping other people to train their dogs and it seemed a natural progression for me to take training classes of my own. After taking a training course for Dog Handler Instructors at the International Animal Behaviour Training College, under the wonderful Angela White, I took my training to the next level and Scamp's School of Dog Training was born, named after a Patterdale cross that I had rescued from a rehoming centre, who was labelled as 'misbehaving' (the only dog out of three hundred that was!). Scamp went on to become a great stooge dog, competed at agility, had magazine articles written about him and frequently took part in dog shows and exhibitions as a demonstration dog.

Whilst 'Scamps' was in its infancy, a knock on the front door brought a concerned neighbour and fellow animal lover, desperate to know if we were aware of anyone who would take in an aggressive Staffie. We opened our door, and very soon our hearts to Buster, a Staffordshire Bull Terrier with serious aggression issues, brought about by bad experiences as a pup and awful handling for the first seven years of his life. Buster would turn from a loving, affectionate pet into a writhing, aggressive beast whenever any other dog came within about a hundred feet of him. Clearly, a whole load more expertise was needed in addressing such a deep-seated reaction, but I was convinced that the same principles would apply and worked tirelessly with him, rewarding only the good behaviours.

Early on in Buster's rehabilitation, I attended courses held by the Institute of Modern Dog Training which centred around the handling and rehabilitation of aggressive dogs. I also travelled all around the country to watch other trainers who worked with such cases. I began to see that it actually was possible to turn around such extreme responses and revert a seriously reactive dog into one that could be trusted around other sociable dogs. In fact, Buster became a stooge dog for other aggressive dogs. This brute climbed into bed alongside Scamp after only a week and they rarely spent any time apart. He became a wonderful example of what can be achieved by kind, reward based methods relying only on positive training methods and basic counter conditioning.

This rapidly became my subject of expertise and my work became recognised by the local council, who invited me to work with poorly trained, reactive dogs and indeed, any in the area deemed to have issues. The council was forward thinking enough to realise that employing me at this stage would save them a great deal of cost and bad publicity further down the line, should there be a spate of dog attacks, due to poor socialisation and a lack of affordable training.

A few years later, after having qualified as a behaviourist and a lot more studying, I relocated to the Midlands and set up the business from scratch once more. It wasn't long before I was working seven days a week, taking referrals from just about every vet for miles around, began training disability assistance dogs, school dogs to aid pupils with special needs, started scent work workshops, ran training seminars as well as training classes and behavioural consults. I was accepted as a member of both the PPG and PPN and passed my assessments and practical exams to become a member of the APDT and even became registered by the Animal Behaviour & Training Council.

Throughout my incredible journey, my thirst for knowledge concerning dog training and behaviour has never been quenched and so I have read countless books on how to train dogs. Some that in my opinion should be banned, some that are just plain wrong, some that are acceptable and some that are inspiringly brilliant, but I have never come across a basic dog training book that describes how to teach your dog from the basics to the more advanced commands, whilst explaining the 'why' and 'how' as well as the progressions and when to change the rewarding regime to improve responses. This allows the reader to understand the theory and therefore, use the same principles to teach your dog to action other cues that are not in the book. Hence, the urge to write and publish my first book and then rewrite and publish, 'The Scamp's Way'.

Repetition!

Association!

Progression!

Introduction

This book is intended as a guide on how to train your dog to action the basic cues such as sit, down and stay, through to walking on a loose lead and more advanced commands. If you read and follow the basic theory chapter and apply this throughout the various sections of the book you will, with practise, have a well-behaved, well-mannered canine companion that you can be proud of. I must just stress that even the best training guides are no substitute for dog training classes. I would advocate a multi-pronged approach. By this I mean combining this book with classes held by a well-researched trainer, and socialisation with as many other dogs and humans as possible. I will discuss how to ensure the trainer is educated in, and understanding of what is required by your dog, and not just a club trainer who has watched a bit of the so called 'Dog Whisperer' and would replicate his cruelty on your dog.

As an educated and successful trainer and behaviourist myself, I would strongly discourage employing any trainer still using or quoting 'dominance', or 'pack based' methods that unfortunately are still being used, as dog training is still largely unregulated.

There is no need for any use of aversion, aversive techniques or aversive tools in dog training and certainly plenty of risk from doing so.

At this point, I realise that many of you will be scratching your heads in puzzlement. What, you're probably thinking, is classed as 'aversive'? We consider this to mean anything that makes our dog uncomfortable, scared or under pressure to do something. It refers to any reprimand or pressure (verbal or physical), a pet corrector spray, water gun or any type of collar designed to deliver an electric shock to the dog at the will of the handler or trainer. Even the once widely used choke chain collar or half choker has no place in this modern time where we now see the catastrophic effect these may have on your dog.

Positive only, reward-based training makes learning fun and rewarding for your dog to progress and so he will become hungry to succeed and learn, making training enjoyable and successful for you both!

Finally, please don't think I am being sexist as I refer to your dog as a 'he' or 'him'. I guess I'm just too lazy to keep retyping 'him/her' or 'his/hers'. In my defence, at the time of writing the first version of this book, my dogs had all been male. Hence, it has become second nature for me to write 'him' or 'his'. None of the methods I talk about in this book are gender specific, and this approach should cover all aspects involved in training any dog; reward based training is effective for all sexes and breeds.

The Theory

Quite recently, I was asked to assess an over excited Border Collie rescue dog, who was very 'bouncy' and jumped up at the new owners' grandchildren to such an extent that they were afraid for the children's safety. They were now questioning their decision to offer the Collie a home, feeling that the only safe and reasonable option was to return the poor boy to the rehoming centre.

After an hour of basic training, an explanation of why the dog was behaving in such a way and guidance on how to implement the methods described in this book to modify the dog's behaviour, we introduced the grandchildren into the room with the dog. After witnessing a couple of minutes of calm demeanour from this usually overly energetic pet, a very emotional grandmother proclaimed, "It is like a miracle!"

I replied, "It is not a miracle, it is simply warm sausage and a basic understanding of learning theory and their reaction to positive reinforcement!"

This might sound over simplistic, but I promise you it is not. The basic theory of training is as follows:

When the dog gets it right, good things happen to him.

If nothing happens to him when he gets it wrong, getting it right becomes the natural choice!

In some cases of behavioural modification, we may extend this to removing the reward for the wrong behaviour, whilst we reward the wanted behaviours, for example, we may walk away from a dog that is exhibiting inappropriate, attention seeking barking (teaching him that barking removes the attention) and then reward the quiet.

Training in a nutshell is achieved by luring a dog into a particular action with a treat, whether that be a morsel of food or a toy. When the dog completes the action, we simply release the treat, and therefore reward him for executing that particular action. Providing we repeat this process, the dog will soon associate this action or behaviour with earning a reward and will offer the action freely. At this stage, we can add a cue.

Then the most important aspect of training a dog. Pretend you have food in your hand if required and ask the dog to carry out the task and then feed from the OTHER hand or have it appear from a treat pouch behind you. By doing this, the dog learns, fast, that if he follows the cue there is a possibility of the 'good stuff' happening if he follows your instruction.

If we don't incorporate this stage, all we have is a dog that follows food and a dog that is unlikely to follow the cue when there is no food on display.

All that's left, is to then progress the action (or shape it) until it is as we would want it.

By using this method your dog will rapidly come to understand that training means the possibility of treats and he will become hungry to learn.

Further down the line we will reduce the treats in order to get better, sharper, quicker responses. This is called scheduled reinforcement and we will go into more detail later in the book.

Positive, reward based training is fun for all involved and as a result your dog will learn a whole lot quicker without the risk of you losing your special bond and the dog 'shutting down' or becoming reactive, which the old fashioned ideas, such as yanking on a choke chain frequently lead towards.

More importantly, the dog learns that when he follows his owner's cues, the 'good stuff' happens. Not only does he then follow the cues, but he wants to be given instruction. When that happens, it is magical as being told what to do becomes a reward and that makes training a doddle!

Dog Training...........

The Good,
the Bad
and
the Ugly

*(and when I say ugly, I mean
down right abusive)*

Good, Modern Ethical Training Vs. Old School Balanced Training

When it comes to training, we used to believe in the carrot and stick. Thankfully times have changed, mainly down to the advance of science, research and an updated understanding of brain chemistry. Using aversion in training is not only less efficient than using reward, but totally unnecessary. I train dogs to be fully accredited Disability Assistance dogs with full public access, meaning they have to be perfect in public. If I can train dogs to this standard without abusing dogs, there is definitely no excuse for the use of chokers, half chokers, electric collars and so on in companion dog training. Yet there are still dog trainers who have never been formally educated in their trade and so rely on suppressing unwanted behaviours, rather than training the wanted ones. These so-called trainers have reinvented the description of this dated and abusive way of controlling a dog. They now call themselves '*balanced*' trainers.

Please do not get drawn in. '*Balanced Training*' is a term used by uneducated dog trainers to excuse abuse within their training methods!

The use of *'balanced training'* is forbidden by EVERY reputable dog training association in the country, the new Dog Training Charter and just about every formally educated trainer in the country. No trainer with a recent formal education in dog training or behaviour will use aversion when training. We hear a lot of trainers describe themselves as 'balanced' trainers. It is no more than a self-descriptive term that has been used by old-school or uneducated trainers to justify using aversive techniques in dog training, just as choke chains were rebranded as 'check chains', when the public realised that the purpose of the tool was in the name.

This was excusable twenty years ago as we really did not know any better. However, science has moved on and as a result so has our working knowledge of brain chemistry. This has been a game changer in dog training and so the plethora of dog training educational suppliers (i.e. the places where dog trainers learn their trade) have all changed how they teach trainers. Further to this, *ALL* reputable dog training associations have a policy not to allow their members to use positive punishment (adding an aversive action to reduce the frequency of an unwanted behaviour). This is not because they want all their members to be warm, fluffy and liked by the dogs. It is for several good reasons including the risks, the lack of long term efficacy compared to positive and reward based dog training, the potential damage and the reduced ability of the dog's learning as a result of these dated methods.

Dog training is not about forcing the dog into new behaviours, it is about motivating the dog to want to carry out the behaviours when you ask for them.

Relationship building, confidence and enjoyment is the key to success. The team shown on the front cover is Emma and her disability assistance dog, Luna. Luna came to me initially to be assessed for her suitability for assistance dog training. When Emma took Luna into her life, the dog was emaciated, had never had any training, not even owned her own collar or lead and was rescued from a concrete back yard whilst pregnant. Within eighteen months she was not only an ADUK accredited assistance dog with full public access but happily goes to Emma's workplace every day with her. Her achievements were recognised when she and Emma were asked to carry the torch for the Commonwealth.

Luna has never been reprimanded, scolded, worn a choke chain, half choker or a slip lead and yet has reached this absolute pinnacle of dog behaviour.

This following picture perfectly depicts the communication, mutual trust, respect, teamwork, etc. that defines the relationship that these two have built during Luna's training.

Further to this, the outdated theory that applying punishment to stop unwanted behaviours relies on applying pain, discomfort or fear (if we didn't apply pain, discomfort or fear, punishment would not work so don't let a balanced trainer tell you 'It's only a half-choker, it won't hurt the dog' - if that was the case, it would have no effect on the dog's behaviour). As it is not in any way necessary to yank a lead, use a choke chain, half choker, slip lead, stamp a foot, pop the lead, shout at the dog, that means these methods are nothing more than applying pain, discomfort or fear unnecessarily to an animal and that, by definition is abuse.

As I previously mentioned, no reputable dog training association will permit their members to use these techniques that so-called 'balanced trainers' use. The IMDT (Institute of Modern Dog Training) requires trainers not only to be assessed but to prove their CPD (continual professional development) and so prove that they are bang up to date with their learning and knowledge of dog behaviour as well as ensuring that no aversive techniques are used. The KCAI (Kennel Club Accredited Instructors Scheme) are the same, with trainers having to pass written, oral and practical exams proving that their members only use positive and motivational methods as well as CPD. Any hint of lead yanking, choker, stamping feet, etc., and they will not be accepted by the association.   APDT (Association of Professional Dog Trainers) was founded in 1993 by Ian Dunbar, PhD, BVetMed, MRCVS and a personal hero of mine. As a renowned veterinarian, animal behaviourist, dog trainer and writer, Dr. Dunbar created the APDT as an inclusive forum for trainers to network with each other and provide educational opportunities and grow the profession.

APDT members undergo a rigorous assessment of both theoretical and practical knowledge and are committed to using kind, fair and effective training methods when teaching dogs and their owners. All members work in accordance with a Code of Practice, which prohibits them from using aversive training methods.

They state clearly on their website, '**Training dogs has changed immensely** in the last few years. It is no longer necessary, or acceptable, to use harsh methods in training, and the use of **gentle, motivational methods** is as successful as they are enjoyable to use.'

The PPG (Pet Professional Guild) and PPN (Pet Professional Network), both provide a huge resource for dog trainers and behaviourists and again, will not permit members to use these 'balanced' harsh or aversive methods.

So why, if all this information is available, do trainers still choose to go down the 'balanced' route?

The answer is quite simply they are not educated, do not keep up to date with recent learning or have not attended any reputable training establishments to learn their trade.

There is a good reason that you will not find a reputable association affiliated balanced trainer; if they were to join an association, they would have to prove their knowledge of learning theory and dog behaviour and if they had that knowledge, they would not use aversive methods and so could brag they were positive only!

Using punishment to suppress an unwanted behaviour (e.g., yanking a lead in an attempt to stop a dog pulling on the lead) is simply a result of the trainer not knowing how to teach a dog the required behaviour (e.g. teaching a dog to walk on a loose lead).

Hence, it is critical that when you are sourcing a trainer, you ask what qualification they have, where they trained, which college or educational provider did they attend and most important of all, do they train the dogs the wanted behaviours or do they wait for the dog to exhibit the unwanted ones and then punish the dog (hoping the dog doesn't misassociate). Quite simply, it is no different taking your dog to a 'balanced' trainer than it is having a heart transplant carried out by someone who never went to medical school, has had no medical training, but claims they know what they are doing because they are carrying out operations the way they always have done and somebody, who also was untrained, showed them how to do it, 20 years ago!

The question should be, why have they not bothered to educate themselves in their trade? I can only think of a few reasons, I am sure you can think of more:

• They are unwilling to pay out for or are not in a position to fund their own education, despite being happy to take your money to teach you.

• Learning how to train a dog effectively and ethically requires an admission that they were wrong in the past, and that can be too hard for many harsh trainers to accept.

• Bullying. Many balanced trainers like bullying and proving they can suppress a behaviour in an animal. There is a link between child abuse and animal abuse but that is a massive topic for another day.

• I would like to say they do not know any better, but sorry guys, that doesn't stack up anymore, as EVERY dog trainer sees QUALIFIED &

FORMALLY EDUCATED TRAINERS on Facebook every single day achieving better results without harsh and aversive treatment of the dogs. Hence, the 'balanced trainers' are CHOOSING to abuse the dogs in their care and worse still, advise their clients to do the same.

The next question should be why if these methods are so bad, are trainers allowed to operate without qualifications, affiliations or allowed to use these so-called 'balanced' methods?

The simple answer is our MPs spent 3 years arguing about whether we should leave or stay in the European Union. Regardless of your personal belief on the subject, the three years of squabbling resulted in everything political being postponed creating a delay on all proposed legislation. There was, however, a charter that was passed through parliament that states that all trainers must not use these aversive methods, but in its first passing it is presently a voluntary charter. For more info see www.dogcharter.uk. It WILL be passed into law, and when it is, the balanced or uneducated dog trainers will have no choice but to enter the 21st century and not only learn their trade, but prove they have a modern understanding and are prepared to work in an ethical and kind manner or not be allowed to operate. In the meantime, ensure that any trainer you wish to employ shows off this logo on their website.

It has already come into law in any establishment that offers day care, whether at home or in a business venue. In order to offer dog day care, you must apply for a licence from the local council and it is a condition of the licence that any training carried out at the premises is 'motivational' only. In other words, positive and reward based. No lead popping, shouting, stamping feet, etc.

So we are getting there, albeit slowly.

So why is it so wrong to use 'balanced' or punishment based training with our dogs?

Here are just a few of the reasons, some basic and some more technical:

- Many years ago, in the dark ages of dog training, we based all our training on the premise that if we rewarded a behaviour, the frequency of the behaviour would increase (very true) and if we punished a behaviour, the frequency would decrease and so we used a combination of both reinforcement and punishment. The carrot and the stick, if you like. However, we now know that if we create sufficient pain, discomfort, fear or association of any of them to deter a dog from repeating a behaviour, the dog will release cortisol in the brain. Cortisol is the fight/flight chemical that changes how we think when threatened in order to help us run away or see off any scary trigger. Once the cortisol level reaches a stress point, there will be a reaction of some description. The cortisol does not have to reach the stress point to create issues in training. Cortisol hampers the neuron highway in the hippocampus part of the brain that controls memory (both recalling and scribing to the long term memory). This is why, if you are not used to public speaking and you have to make a speech at a wedding or you attend a job interview, you can practise what you are going to say over and over, but your mind still goes blank when you start talking. In canine terms, this means that as soon as you apply enough punishment to affect the dog's behaviour, the dog's ability to learn new behaviours is severely restricted.

- Once the cortisol builds up in the brain, the dog will automatically go into a high alert status (just as you would if someone started yanking you around by your necklace); the dog will focus and then associate the punishment with the trigger being present, and this will NOT be his behaviour. An example of this is a dog that I work with on a regular basis, which when I started working with her freaked out on sight of a walking stick. This was deep rooted from when in pup class the trainer would 'tap' the dogs with his stick when they exhibited unwanted behaviours. Never in a month of Sundays would the poor dog ever associate being hit with a walking stick with having to stop typical pup behaviours. Instead, she learnt bad things happen when someone approaches with a walking stick. The common mis-association is bad things happen in classes when there are other dogs about and so dogs become suspicious when there are other dogs present.

- If the cortisol builds up enough, there will be a stress response. Not long ago, a dog that frequented the same training school as the above dog that was hit with a walking stick on a pup course, bit its owner in class. There was nothing wrong with the dog, it simply had not been taught how to behave around other dogs and so pulled towards them. Rather than teach the dog to ask permission to approach, the owner was instructed (disgustingly) to remove the harness and replace it with a half choker and a secondary collar that squirted water when activated remotely by the trainer's assistant. The dog then choked and had water in its face every time it pulled towards another dog. The dog had absolutely no idea why it was choking and having a blast of water in its face regularly and so the logical part of the brain disengaged, and the fight/flight part of the brain was activated. The dog could not get away and so reacted in a way that we call 'deflection' and bit the owner.

- Another dog came to me after being thrown out of another class after biting the trainer for 'no reason'. The previous week the dog (who had not been taught to settle quietly) was barking in class and so the trainer squirted the poor dog in the face with a water pistol. She repeated this every time the dog barked. The following week, she went to stroke the dog and the dog grabbed her hand in its mouth and would not let go.   Strangely enough, the dog had related the water pistol with the trainer's hand and not his barking......who would have thought?

- There are two ways of teaching a dog to sit. The old school way of saying 'sit' and pushing the dogs back end down will work as the dog will learn to get his backside on the floor to avoid the punishment of having a hand push down on his back.   However, the dog will not want to be told to sit due to the negative associations it will have made whilst learning.   If taught the correct way by luring with food and rewarding, then progressing to following the cue for the possibility of something good, not only will the dog sit on cue, but he will want to be told what to do and so will be more likely to choose to follow instruction in future.

- The most important aspect of training a dog is the mutual respect and bond. I don't need to tell you how our bond would go, if every time you came to my class, I yanked you by your necklace or choked you when you got it wrong!

Think about this scenario; you have a young child starting school.   To avoid chaos at lunchtime, the school decides that all pupils must walk on the left hand side of the corridors.   Rather than teach the kids which side is left and teach them to walk on that side, the teachers just stand in the corridor and smack the children when they stray on to the right hand side of the corridor.   Would this teach the kids to walk on the left? Of course not, most of the kids would just learn they get smacked when teachers are about and so would avoid teachers, destroying any trust. Others would associate the smacks with being in the corridor and so would avoid corridors.   Some would become violent and react to the teachers with aggression.   There would also be some that would become anxious and develop mental health issues.   I am sure that if you discovered that the teachers were smacking your children for unwanted behaviours, without teaching the kids the wanted ones, you would have the teacher prosecuted at the very least and yet...........we still have so-called balanced trainers yanking a dog's neck or choking a dog for pulling on a lead without teaching the dog what is expected of it or motivating the dog to do it.

If a trainer uses methods that include the use of pain or fear (such as slip leads, choke chains, half chokers, prong collars, etc.) you need to be asking are they using pain and fear in their training because they don't know how to train without them, or do they know how to train without using pain or fear and choose to anyway. Either response should be enough for you to run a mile!

My ultimate hero is Dr Ian Dunbar, who made this famous quote about the use of shock collars. It is also true for choke chains, half chokers, prong collars, no pull harnesses, pet correctors or any other piece of abusive equipment designed to cause pain or fear to a dog.

"To use shock as an effective dog training method you will need:

- *A thorough understanding of canine behaviour.*
- *A thorough understanding of learning theory.*
- *Impeccable timing.*

And if you have those three things, you don't need a shock collar."

There is Nothing

More Rewarding

in Life

than

Being Rewarded!

Rewarding Behaviour

Reward based training is easy, all we have to do is reward the wanted behaviour, right? However, have you considered the effect of the quality of the reward? How the dog perceives the quality? What about frequency of rewarding? If we are using food, is there a time when the reward will be more effective? How does the value of a reward affect how the action is scribed onto the memory? If we stop rewarding, will the wanted behaviour cease? Can we over reward? *And so on, and so on, and so on!*

It is easy to overlook the importance of how and when to reward.

In a nutshell, we use the highest value reward we can and reward the dog as much as possible when we start training. Once the dog expects the 'good stuff' for getting it right, we reduce the frequency of the rewards to improve the response (whether that be speed, quality or attitude). The reduction of frequency of rewards is carried out progressively and we may reward every second correct execution of a task or reward every 10 seconds of a loose lead walk rather than every 5 seconds. This is called 'scheduled reinforcement' and there are several methods.

If a dog believes he will get a lump of chicken every time he sits on cue, regardless of quality or speed, there is no incentive to sit accurately or quickly. If we only reward fifty percent of the tasks (a 'fixed rate scheduled reinforcement'…. but more of the techy stuff later) and go one step further and only reward the best fifty percent of the responses, the dog will naturally improve the response in order to achieve the reward.

Let's start at the beginning. What is a reward? Quite simply, it is anything that creates a positive emotional response in our brain for achieving a wanted task or behaviour. It could be food, a play with a toy, fuss or even the pleasure of pleasing the person who asked for the behaviour.

A game with a toy such as a tug with a 'ball on a rope' can be a great reward for any 'high drive' dog, like a Malinois or a German Shepherd, but you are limited on repetition training. When working with a high drive dog that loves a ball, I keep a ball on a rope in my pocket and reward with food for the repetition. Then when the dog offers a really good response (e.g., working on recall and the dog comes away from playing with a load of other doggy friends for the first time on cue) out comes the ball for a game as a BONANZA reward.

Fuss is good (whether verbal or touch) and something that we probably all reward our dogs with, without realising. How many times a day do you say, 'Good boy' or 'Good girl' to your pet?

However, food is king. It is easy to use, we can use it for multiple repetition and we can change the value of the rewards by simply changing the food (see Hierarchy of Treats). It is convenient to carry around and generally will trump any other reward.

'My Dog is not food motivated!'

I hear this on an almost daily basis, however if the dog is not underweight, it is very definitely food motivated. It is simply just not enjoying the treats in that particular scenario or environment. If the dog is not taking treats, we really need to find out why and address those issues, as it could be a symptom of a more serious problem.

If you consider your dog not to be food motivated, do look at the following possible causes and solutions.

Poor Diet – Most branded, pet shop and supermarket branded foods are of poor quality and are bulked out with fillers, such as grains (in particular, wheat or maize) which not only negatively affects the dog's longevity and welfare but can affect how the dog sees food. Visit www.allaboutdogfood.co.uk and ensure it scores over ninety percent. The website is accurate and good. As a trainer, I can spot a dog on poor food, just as I can spot a dog on a good diet. Just because a food is recommended by a vet, breeder or pet shop, it does not make it a good food. It generally tells us who is sponsoring them or offering them the biggest 'kickback' or bribe.

Over Arousal – the dog is too excited and over aroused to take the treats (common when the dog first goes into a training class full of other exciting dogs). Train, where you can, in a less exciting environment and introduce the distractions slowly. If you are teaching recall in a field full of dogs and the dog is not taking the treats because he is over aroused by the other dogs, move him away from the other dogs, give him time to settle and start away from the triggers that over aroused him. Once the dog is used to taking the treat for the behaviour, reintroduce the distractions/triggers in small increments over a period of time.

Anxiety – Anxiety suppresses appetite. If you consider your dog to be anxious in an environment, remove him from it as soon as possible and employ a behaviourist to work with your dog. Anxiety rarely improves on its own, generally will worsen and often leads to reactivity. Signs to look out for are any of the following; rapid blinking, yawning, diverting gaze, tail down more than normal, whale eye (you can see the white at the side of your dog's eyes), lip licking, ears going backwards more than normal, etc.

Treat Value too Low – Teaching a dog focus is easy in the house, where there is nothing new or overly exciting and so most of the time you can use the dog's kibble. However, if you are teaching a fast recall away from other dogs, a piece of the dog's normal everyday diet kibble is not going to cut the mustard. In this case, up the value, warm up some ox liver or a use a piece of cooked mackerel. So often in class, clients are amazed when their dog is ignoring them but will perform exceptionally for me, simply because my treats are new and smelly and their treats are boring and over used.

Dog's Food Left Down for the Dog to Freegraze – This is so commonly the reason for a dog's poor performance training wise. If a dog doesn't eat his meal, it should be lifted. If we don't, the dog will learn to pick at the food throughout the day, meaning he will never eat it when he is hungry and with it being there all the time, the value of food will drop to zero.

Do you like Thornton's Chocolates? Of course you do.....everybody does. If I was to pop round your house twice a day with a box of Thornton's and offer you a few chocolates, you would enjoy them today, tomorrow and every day that I continued to come round with my generous behaviour. However, if I was to come around your house and put a dustbin size container in the middle of your lounge and fill it to the top with the chocolates and then come around twice a day and just fill the container back up to the top, you would grab a chocolate every time you passed the bin for a day. Tomorrow, you would enjoy them a little less and by the end of the week, you would be so fed up with them, you would most likely ignore them totally.

I once worked at a bakery that made triple chocolate muffins. Part of my job was actually to keep tasting them throughout the day. I promise you, if I ever have to eat another muffin, it will be too soon.

When something is available in the environment all the time, the value drops.

If you want to look at it from an economics perspective, a continual supply without a continual demand will result in a decrease of value of the product.

If you are still not convinced and you have teenage children, put a bowl of ten pound notes on the dining table and tell your kids to help themselves, whenever they want some money. Keep topping it up twice a day. After a week, ask the kids if they would like to clean your car for a fiver and wait for the response!

Hierarchy of Treats

An exercise well worth doing with your dog is to choose five treats that you think your dog will respond to, such as mackerel cake, liver cake, commercial dog treats, kibble from your dog's dinner and a toy. Have the dog sit in front of you and have one treat in one hand and a different treat in your other hand, slowly move them around the front of your dog's face, allowing him to smell each and then hold them either side of your dog and make a note of which one he takes first. This will tell you which of the two treats are of the higher value to your dog. Repeat this with all the treats and you will soon be able to record a hierarchy of treats (as below) for your own dog. Please bear in mind that it will be different for different dogs.

Scamp's Hierarchy of Treats

1. *Ball*
2. *Liver Cake*
3. *Mackerel Cake*
4. *Commercial Dog Treat*
5. *Kibble*

Buster's Hierarchy of Treats

1. *Mackerel Cake*
2. *Liver Cake*
3. *Commercial Dog Treat*
4. *Ball*
5. *Kibble*

When teaching a dog a recall from distractions, don't bother with the lower ranked treats, go with the high ones from the off. Keep the repetitions down and go high value.

When basic obedience training such as teaching sit, down, etc., start with a low value treat. As he starts to get bored or less responsive, move on to a higher value treat and he should perk up. Again, as he gets bored of that one, move further up the hierarchy. **Note:** *Starting with the highest value treat means if he gets bored of it, you have nowhere to go!*

When to Reward

This is critical! Reward any behaviour you want to see more of. If the dog sits on cue, reward him. If he lies down and settles under the table at the local pub, reward him. If he ignores a squirrel and focusses on you, reward him. When you have a pup or start training an adult dog, reward, reward, reward. You cannot over reward at this stage. When you start training, reward everything you possibly can (except for the bad stuff, obviously). At this stage of training, I genuinely couldn't care less if the dog displays a good sit or can do a ten minute 'out of sight' stay. What I am looking for is that the dog learns good stuff happens when they follow Mum or Dad's cue.

The more we reward the dog for following cues in many different environments, the more the dog will want to be told what to do and that is when the dog becomes compliant. Not only does the dog become more compliant but will enjoy it.

The added bonus is the dog will start to look for instruction in unfamiliar circumstances, rather than acting independently.

Happy Dog, Happy Handler

That said, once the dog is following our cues, we don't want to carry on carrying a shed load of food around with us and feeding the dog every time he does what is expected of him, so we start reducing the rewards. Most of the time a 'Good boy' will suffice to keep the behaviour from becoming 'extinct'. We will also want to sharpen up any response. This is also achieved by reducing the frequency of the rewards.

If your boss was to pay you the same wage whether you performed at one hundred percent and went above and beyond or whether you simply did the minimum necessary to get through the day, it wouldn't be long before the quality of your work dipped. It is no different with our dogs. If they think they will get paid whether they come back instantly or in their own time, there is no motivation for improving the speed of the recall.

To counteract this, we incorporate something called 'Scheduled Reinforcement'.

Scheduled Reinforcement

Scheduled reinforcement is usually defined as rewarding good behaviours, but not every time. Either randomly (but keeping an eye on averages) or rewarding to a pattern, as opposed to rewarding every time the dog 'gets it right' (although purists can argue that rewarding every time is effectively a fixed schedule reinforcer, simply with a fixed ratio of 1:1).

When teaching a new behaviour, we reward every correct execution of a task and then convert to scheduled reinforcement, when the dog knows what is expected from him.

There are many types of schedules for rewarding. The following are some examples:

Fixed Ratio Schedules – 1 reward per fixed number of correct actions or behaviours.

Variable Ratio Schedules – 1 reward per differing number of correct actions or behaviours but the average rate is measured.

Fixed Interval Schedules – 1 reward for several correct behaviours but the rewards are separated by a fixed period of time.

Variable Interval Schedules – 1 reward for several correct behaviours with the rewards separated by differing periods of time, but the average time will be measured.

Saying that, I would suggest that you ignore all the technical stuff or trying to count or time the intervals and simply just reward the best fifty percent of correct behaviours. That way your dog will continue to improve the response as he only gets rewarded for the improved action.

The Advanced Bits

When you reward a behaviour, you create a positive emotional response in the hippocampus part of the brain. It is the hippocampus that controls the transference of data from the working memory to the long-term memory. The bigger the emotion, the harder it is scribed to the long-term memory. In other words, the higher the value of the treat, the quicker the dog will learn.

This is one of the reasons that so-called 'balanced' training is nothing like as effective as reward based training. In order to use aversive methods to train a dog, you have to create a negative emotional response in the brain to deter the dog from repeating the unwanted behaviour. However, when you create a negative emotional response in the brain, the dog perceives it as a threat and releases cortisol (the anxiety or fight/flight hormone). Cortisol hampers the neuron highway in the hippocampus to encourage the brain to make decisions from the fast acting amygdala part of the brain. When you hamper the hippocampus, you hamper the transference of information to the long term memory. In other words, when you use aversion, it is harder for the dog to learn, which is not in any way conducive for training efficacy.

Remember- If a dog is not doing what we want him to do, it is for one of two reasons – Either the dog does not know what is expected of him or he is not motivated enough to do it.

If it is because the dog does not know what is expected of him, that is down to our training method. If it is down to lack of motivation, then that is down to how we are rewarding the behaviour!

The Three Stages of Dog Training

1.   *Repetition*

2.   *Association*

3.   *Progression*

Repetition
Achieve the action, usually by lure with a treat (avoiding any physical pressure on the dog) and repeat until the dog freely offers the behaviour for the treat.

Association
This is the stage where we have the dog associate the good stuff with following the cue. Hence, he associates completing the action or behaviour with receiving a reward. We then add a cue, whether that be a verbal cue, a whistle or a visual cue and the dog then associates the action with the cue, rather than just following the lure.

The most important factor of this stage is to ensure the dog associates that it is following the cue that pays and not simply following the food. If we are teaching a dog to sit (see the next section), we will position a treat and move our hand so the dog follows the food and performs the 'sit'. Once repeated several times, we do it again, but with no food in our hand. The dog will expect there to be food in the hand and will follow the hand into the correct position and we then feed from the other hand that was behind our back. This way the dog associates following the cue as a good thing and not just simply following the food. If we don't create this association, we have a dog that just follows food, meaning when we haven't got treats or there is something more rewarding in the environment, the dog will most likely ignore us.

Progression

The most important stage! Once a dog has learned a new action, the training does not end there. Progressing the behaviour until it is exactly as we want it, and it becomes a learned behaviour (i.e. it follows the command by cue, rather than making a choice) is as important as teaching the dog the task in the first place. We also want to progress the command so the dog will offer the behaviour when it is required without you even having to perform the cue (for example we can teach a dog to sit on command, but it is far more practical if the dog sits in front of you automatically when you get his lead out, or he sits by your side, every time you stop at a kerb on his walk).

I often ask handlers in the first class of my bronze course, 'Whose dogs sit on cue'? Everybody in the class will smugly put a hand in the air, without fail. I then ask them, 'So when your dog is fifty meters away in a field playing with twenty other dogs and you shout out, 'Sit', how quick does his bottom hit the floor?' This is the point that the hands drop back down and I explain that actually the dogs do not sit on cue, they actually only sit on cue up to a level of distraction. The level of distraction that they will follow the cue to depends on how far you have progressed the training of that cue. We always want to progress that level of training past the levels of distraction that the dog is likely to experience. It is no good having a dog that walks nicely on a loose lead providing there are no other dogs about or a dog that will recall providing there are no squirrels in the park and so on.

Best Way to

Achieve Top Marks

is with

Top 'Marking'

Marking the Right Behaviour

It is critical when training a dog that we can 'mark' the right behaviour, often described as taking a snapshot of the desired task, but what is it we are talking about and why is it so important?

Basically, we know that if we reward any behaviour we will increase the frequency of that behaviour. However, it is imperative that the dog understands what he is being rewarded for. Not a problem if we are teaching a dog to sit, as we can pretty much get the reward in to the dog's mouth as soon as his backside hits the deck. Not so easy if we are teaching the dog a 'send away' for example. If the dog's mouth is not next to your hand with the food in it, there will be a delay between him completing the action and you rewarding him for it. The longer the delay, the less likely the dog is to associate the action with the treat; we need to mark the behaviour as it happens and so we use either a marker word or a clicker. They work exactly the same, except a clicker is obviously more consistent than our voice.

The following is an explanation of why and how we mark a behaviour with a clicker but do remember that we can use a marker word such as 'good' or 'yes' instead of clicking a clicker. Using a marker word, let's face it is a lot less hassle in the practical sense than carrying around a clicker (we need 3 pairs of hands as it is to carry our water bottle, poo bags, long line, various treats and so on).

If you are going to use a marker word, pick a word and stick to it. I use 'good'. **DO NOT USE 'GOOD BOY'**. You are after a short sharp sound and you will overuse 'good boy', you say it all day long, 'Come get your dinner, there's a *good boy*', 'I'm off to work now, so you be a *good boy*', 'Be a *good boy* for the dog walker', etc., etc. Then for best effect comply with the following instructions, but simply replace, where it says 'click', with your marker word.

In my opinion, the clicker is the greatest invention of all time. It enables us to train a dog efficiently and effectively in a fraction of the time that traditional methods do. It was a method that was popularised by former dolphin and killer whale trainer, Karen Prior. (I strongly recommend that anyone who owns, works with or trains dogs, reads her book, 'Don't Shoot the Dog').

We all know that by rewarding a dog's behaviour, we are increasing the probability of him repeating that behaviour, and the most effective way of rewarding a dog is to feed him high value edible treats. Timing is key; the more quickly the food arrives in the dog's mouth after the dog has exhibited the wanted behaviour, the more likely he is to make the association between the reward and the behaviour. That is where we can fall short. Also, if we are looking at positional work such as heelwork, if we have food in our hand, the chances are the dog is likely to be drawn to the treat. Hence, by the time we have fed him, he is in a different position to the one that we wanted him to be rewarded for. What is more frustrating is trying to reward the dog for an action when he is not within arm's length of us. This is because by the time we reach him with the treat he has moved towards us, wagged his tail, moved his ears and looked up at us and so, has not got the foggiest idea of what we are rewarding him for. Also, when we are working with a reactive dog and we want to reward him for not reacting to an approaching dog, you can guarantee that by the time you have found your treats and got it to the dog's mouth the distance between the dogs has reduced significantly, your dog has reacted, and you are now rewarding your dog for the unwanted behaviour.

This is where the clicker comes into its own. We use the click of the clicker to mark the exact time that the dog exhibits the wanted behaviour. We can click our dog without having to search our pockets for a treat whilst trying to watch the dog and any stimulus that he may react to.

The only problem is that the dog doesn't know what the click means, so we must teach him. We can do this in ten minutes but for it to be effective, do this over a week as in the process below. By the end of the week the dog will consider the click to be the 'primary' reward and the edible treat will become the 'enforcer' of the reward. This means that when the dog exhibits a wanted behaviour, whether we have asked for it or not we can reward it instantly with a click and then approach the dog with the food. This instant rewarding is not possible without the clicker or a marker word.

In short, the dog will remember the point he was marked for the behaviour, not when the treat arrived in his mouth.

Conditioning the Dog to the Clicker

Day 1 to 3: Precede every treat given to the dog with a click. (Click, then treat every time). At dinner time, click, then give him a kibble. Repeat this a few times, then click and put the bowl on the floor.

Day 4 to 7: Precede every treat with a request for a known behaviour, click on execution, then treat. *For example:* Ask the dog to sit, click the instant his bottom touches the floor, then treat him. Repeat this as often as possible.

By now your dog is fully charged to the clicker and not only regards the click as a reward, but will have learned he gets clicked when he complies with your cues.

You are now ready to really speed up the training process, as you can now efficiently and accurately mark and reward any wanted behaviours. Just remember to follow the click with the treat to keep it working effectively but no rush! You have 10-15 seconds to find that morsel of food from your pocket after a successful click.

If I want my dog to exhibit a particular behaviour, I shouldn't be thinking, 'How can I make him do that?'

I should be thinking, 'How can I make him want to do that?'

How Do I Teach My Dog His Name

Now, this may seem obvious to you, but remember that a dog does not instinctively know his name. In fact, all a name is to a dog is a prompt to look at his handler as there is a cue coming. You need to teach your dog, when he hears his name to pay attention and look up to you in readiness for the instruction. For example, 'Fido...Sit', 'Shaggy....Come', 'Rocky....Stay', etc.

In order to teach him to pay attention when he hears his name, apply the following three steps. (As you work your way through this book, you should start to notice a pattern).

Repetition

With your dog in front of you, hold a treat in front of your face and simultaneously say his name, then without hesitation, as the dog looks at your face (or the food in front of your face), mark it with a 'good' or a click if you are using a clicker, and feed him the treat. Repeat this six times. This is purely to get the dog used to looking into your eyes.

Now we are going to ask you to modify things a wee bit by asking you to hold the treat to the side of your face low enough that your dog can touch it with his nose as you call his name, but you will keep it safe in a closed fist so he cannot get it.

Most importantly, once the treat is not directly in front of your face do not release it. If the treat is held slightly to one side of the face and he continues to stare or mouth at the treat without looking at you, do not let him take it, no matter how much he persists. He will eventually look at you, even if only for a clue on how to win the reward. It may just be a flick of the eyes, but that is enough for you to mark it with a 'good' or click and you can give the dog the treat. Keep repeating this process, but only mark and treat him for making eye contact. He will soon get the hang of it.

A good time to try this is at mealtimes, as dogs are at their most responsive to food, when they are at their hungriest. By using bits of their meal, you do not have to worry about filling your dog up with less nutritious treats.

Association

As your dog begins to associate looking at you with being rewarded with the treat when he hears his name being mentioned, hold the treat out at arm's length, to one side of you and call his name. If he tries to wrestle the treat from your hand, do not release it until he makes eye contact with you. As before, keep repeating until, *bingo*, he looks at you every time you call his name before taking the treat. He now associates his name with giving you his attention. This makes every other command you teach him easier, as you can gain his focus before the next instruction.

Progression

This is an easy progression. If your dog is looking up at you when you call his name as he is sitting by you and your supply of treats, you are ready to start advancing to calling his name when he is not expecting it. For example, as you take him on his daily walks, while he is playing with his toy, etc. (call his name, if he looks up at you, mark it with a 'good' and treat him immediately, if he doesn't, show him the treat and repeat). You can even train it into him whilst he is eating his meal, when he responds to his name and looks up, give him a real high value treat and then leave him to continue his dinner.

What we are looking for is what we call a 'head snap'. This is where the dog involuntarily spins his head around to look at you, when he hears his name mentioned.

What Could Possibly Go Wrong?

Very little can go wrong (famous last words!). However, if your over-zealous pooch starts to jump up when hearing his name, this needs correcting. All you have to do is remain stationary until all four paws are on the ground before you treat him and he will soon learn that he is being rewarded for just his attention and not jumping up.

'Sit Happens!'

How Do I Teach My Dog To Sit

This is the most common task we ask of our dog, and probably the one action that most dogs will demonstrate freely. This is because in the pursuit of reward, the dog will have worked out that this is what has pleased the handler the most. We all encourage our dogs to sit before dinner, at the kerb, for a treat, etc., so it becomes the most common cue that we expect our pet to action. The more a dog repeats any action, the quicker it becomes a learned behaviour and the more reliable the action becomes.

There is a growing campaign on social media started by some dog trainers stating that we shouldn't teach a dog to sit on cue, as it is not a natural position for a dog. I am pretty sure this is just a way of creating controversy and as such, manipulating the social media algorithms. Firstly, it is a very natural position for a dog or even his close relative, the wolf. If you are fortunate enough to have the opportunity to study wild dogs or wolves, the dog on guard will often sit, as this lifts his head higher so he can see further. Secondly, there are far more unnatural things we teach the dog, like walking with a lead attached to him, having the dog walk at our speed, having the dog leave food found on the floor outdoors, but eat out of a bowl indoors and so on. However, we teach the dog these 'unnatural' behaviours so he can fit into and live happily and harmoniously, as well as safely, in our environment.

We should point out at this stage that thankfully the days of pushing down on the dog's back end and demanding he sits are well and truly gone. This dated method will teach the dog to sit by having the dog learn to get his bottom down before it is pushed to the floor, and so learn to avoid the punishment. He will learn to sit but won't want to be told to do so, as it will be associated with having his rear end shoved to the floor. If we teach it force free by luring and rewarding, not only will the dog have learnt to sit on cue but will want his handler to give him instruction as there is the possibility of the 'good stuff' happening….and that is what creates a happy compliant dog.

Repetition

To teach your dog to sit, you quite simply place a treat in between your thumb and middle finger and place it in front of your dog's nose with your palm facing upwards and hold your wrist straight.

Slowly raise the treat up by bending your wrist and moving the treat slowly over the dog's head. His head should then follow the treat, resulting in his bottom going down towards the floor. If you are lucky enough for the dog to go into a 'sit' straight away, mark it with a verbal 'good' or a click the second his bottom touches the floor, and release the treat into the dog's mouth.

It is more likely that you will have to adjust the position of the treat until the dog's head follows your hand into a position that causes him to take up a sitting position. Do not worry if your dog does not take up his sitting position immediately, he will do what he can to work out what he must do to release the treat and should eventually, with a little repositioning of the treat, sit correctly. If his paw comes up delay the treat until all paws are planted on the floor, mark with a 'good' or click and then release the treat.

What is important is to mark the point that the correct sitting position occurs so that the dog realises what he is being treated for.

Next, repeat this several times. The more you repeat it, the sooner the dog will offer the sit position by just the action of curling your hand upwards. (This now becomes the visual signal).

Note: When teaching a new position, we do not say, 'Sit' until the dog is freely offering the sit position for the visual cue. If we start saying, 'Sit' while the dog is in the standing position before the dog understands what is expected of him, we will simply confuse the poor mutt.

Association

Your dog will now be associating sitting with receiving a treat, so at this stage we can add the verbal command, 'sit!'

We continue to repeat the above process but every time we curl our hand into the visual cue, we say 'sit!' so your dog associates the action with the verbal command as well as the visual cue.

The visual cue for 'sit'.

In no time at all, he will be offering his sit every time you either show the visual cue or say the verbal command.

Then for the most important stage of training a dog; you pretend to have food in your hand when you don't while you lure the sit. The dog should follow your hand thinking there is food in it; as he transfers into the sit position, mark it and feed from the other hand (ideally from behind your back or from out of sight). This teaches the dog almost immediately, that if he follows your cue, there is the possibility of the 'good stuff' appearing. *IF WE DON'T CHANGE OVER AND REWARD FROM THE OTHER HAND, THE DOG WILL NOT ASSOCIATE THE GOOD STUFF WITH FOLLOWING THE CUE AND WILL SIMPLY BE A DOG THAT FOLLOWS FOOD.* If the dog only follows the food and not the cue, he probably will not follow your instruction when you have no food or when there is something more interesting than the treat in the environment.

Initially, give your dog a treat every time he successfully sits on command, but over time reduce this to one treat for just the fastest responses (see scheduled reinforcement).

Progression

Once you have your dog presenting a good sit when you ask for one, you can start progressing it. Initially, repeat the process but don't release the treat for a few seconds, and then five seconds and so on. When you do this, you are treating the dog for transferring into the 'sit' position and staying there. This will ensure that when you ask for a 'sit', your dog will comply by sitting and staying there, rather than placing his backside on the floor and getting straight back up.

You can also reverse the cue for a side sit. Have the dog by your side, but this time have your arm down loose with the back of your hand facing forward. Simply curve your hand so your fingertips go upwards over the dog's head, causing the dog to sit facing forward, rather than sitting facing you.

What Could Possibly Go Wrong?

Some dogs, when learning how to sit lift their head when following the treat and shuffle backwards, rather than touch their bottom on the floor. To overcome this, you can place your other hand behind the dog to remove the option of him moving backwards.

Note: *NEVER* put any downwards pressure on any part of your dog. (It is not called force-free training for no reason!). Dogs always learn faster when they get rewarded for making a correct decision, rather than having the decision made for them.

Once your dog has associated the lifting of the hand into the 'sit' visual cue, you can start to practise it from a few feet away and then increase the distance that he responds to. You'll be amazed at how far away you can be from him and still get him to follow your cue.

Teach Sit on Cue

1. Hold a treat between your middle finger and thumb with palm facing upward. Place in front of dog's nose and lift up slowly, so that the dog's head follows the treat upwards. His back end should go the other way and when it touches the floor with both paws staying on the floor, mark and release the treat.

2. Repeat until the dog offers the sit every time you lift the food upwards, then pretend you have food in your hand and lift your hand as previous. The dog will assume you have a treat in your hand and offer the sit. Mark and reward from your other hand so the dog learns to follow the cue and not just the food.

3. Start to shape the visual cue until you just have to move your fingers up to cue the sit.

4. Once (and only when) the dog is offering the sit for the visual cue, start saying, 'Sit' as the dog transitions to the sit position. It won't be long before the dog freely offers a sit for the visual or verbal cue.

5. Reward heavily every time the dog complies so the dog understands that good stuff happens when compliant.

NOTE: Never apply physical pressure on the dog

Going Down Without a Fight........

Isn't Always a Bad Thing!

How Do I Teach My Dog To Lie Down

'Down' is the next obvious step after teaching your dog to sit and is, without doubt, the most important action that you can teach your dog. When your dog will lie down on cue, you will have control over a potentially dangerous situation. He cannot lunge at another dog if he is lying down, nor can he jump in front of an oncoming car, or further excite an aroused dog. This will give you an extra second or so of valuable time to regain control, if required.

It is also the obvious fore runner of the 'emergency down'. Imagine a scenario where the dog is running towards you, when you spot a youth on a bicycle about to cycle between you and the dog. If your dog continues on his present course, there is the very serious risk of a collision with the cyclist, thus a reliable emergency down or stop is essential for the safety of your dog.

Also, if your dog has a high prey drive and spots a cat across a busy road and breaks free, a down-stay is far more reliable than a sit or stand-stay, as it gives you more time to reattach the lead to the harness or the collar.

Repetition (Method 1)

Before you teach your dog to lie down, you need to have him in a good sit position. You then lure him down to a down position with a treat. Using a good quality food treat, place it between your thumb and middle finger, with your fingers as straight as possible and your thumb towards the floor.

Put your hand just under your dog's nose and slowly lower your hand to the floor. If you are really lucky, your dog will go straight down and you can mark it and release the treat the second his chest touches the floor. You repeat this as many times as it takes until he is presenting you with a decent down with you only having to lower a flat hand in front of him.

It is more likely that your dog will try and take the treat from your hand by dropping his head and keeping his chest off the floor. This can usually be resolved by moving the treat in between the dog's front paws, resulting in him having to shuffle backwards resulting in that elusive chest touch down. It may take a little more manoeuvring and patience or even moving the treat to one side of the dog, but your dog will hopefully work it out for himself. Timing is critical, mark and release the treat when, and only when he is lying down with his chest in contact with the ground. Repeat this constantly until he is offering that lie down every time without having to manoeuvre the treat about.

If, however, no amount of tactical moving of the treat around the floor results in your dog lying down, don't panic, there is a second method that I use quite frequently. (Read the 'What Can Possibly Go Wrong?' section).

Association

As for the sit, we then need to have the dog associate the action with the cue and so on with the most important stage of training a dog…..you pretend to have food in your hand when you don't while you lure the dog down. The dog should follow your hand thinking there is food in it, as he transfers into the down position, mark it and feed from the other hand. This teaches the dog almost immediately, that if he follows your cue, there is the possibility of the 'good stuff' appearing. *IF WE DON'T CHANGE OVER AND REWARD FROM THE OTHER HAND, THE DOG WILL NOT ASSOCIATE THE GOOD STUFF WITH FOLLOWING THE CUE AND WILL SIMPLY BE A DOG THAT FOLLOWS FOOD.* If the dog only follows the food and not the cue, he probably will not follow your instruction when you have no food or when there is something more interesting than the treat in the environment.

At this stage, your dog is already associating a tasty reward with lying down, and so we now need to associate the lying down action with a verbal as well as a visual cue. This is simply achieved by saying the command, 'down', as you bring the dog into the lying position and lower your hand. Eventually, your dog will assume the down position every time you either say, 'down', or just show the now visual cue of lowering your hand with your palm faced down.

Once he is performing a good quality down on every cue, reduce the number of times you treat him to once every two successful downs and then every three, etc.

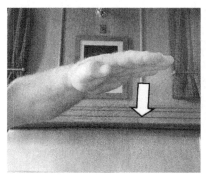 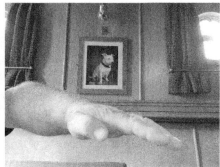

The visual cue for 'down'.

Progression

To progress the quality of the down, mark the behaviour but increase the time between the successful down and treating your dog, thus ensuring when your dog executes a 'down', he doesn't jump straight back up again. This works because you are now rewarding the dog for lying down and staying down.

If he does jump up before he is treated, put him back into the down position before giving him the reward, then go back a step. Ask the dog for a down and release the food as soon as he goes down and then start to increase the delay between the action and the reward.

The next day, you will not take your hand all the way to the floor and from then on, you need to progress the visual cue by showing the flat hand (palm down) and move it just a few inches towards the floor, but each day show the cue a little higher up. Within a relatively short space of time, you will be standing fully erect and having the dog follow the cue without you having to bend down to the floor.

The other good progression is to work on an 'Emergency Down'.

Start with your dog in the sit position and lure him down with a treat.

Release the treat the instant the dog's chest touches the floor.

What Could Possibly Go Wrong?

In many cases, it doesn't matter how long you manoeuvre the treat for, or whichever way you move it, the dog will just not put his chest on the floor, or he puts his chest down, but his backside pops up. This then calls for a little more athletic method:

Repetition (Method 2)

Start by putting your dog into a sit on your left and then crouch down so the back of your thighs are resting on your calves, as if about to start a Russian Cossack dance. Stick your right leg out with your right foot on the floor, creating a 'bridge' with the back of your right thigh being just slightly higher than the depth of your dog's chest.

Hold the treat in your right hand and place it under your knee. As your dog touches the treat bring it slowly back through under your leg, luring your dog under your leg. As the height of your bridge is only slightly over the height of your dog's back, in order for him to follow the lure, his chest has to touch the floor. At that instant, release the reward and treat your dog.

Repeat this until he is doing this fluently, and then remove your leg and try it without your 'bridge'. If he still goes down then proceed to the 'association' stage and introduce the verbal cue. If not, then go back to bridging your leg until he gets the hang of it.

Note: It is possible do this sitting on a chair with one leg forward if you find the 'Cossack dancer' position uncomfortable. You can even lure him under a chair or similar if you can find something that will form a bridge suitable for enticing him into the perfect 'down'.

Make sure you lure your dog under your leg and release the treat as soon as his chest touches the floor. Providing you put no pressure on the dog's back and he is ending up in the down position by choice, he will soon follow the cue without your leg being there!

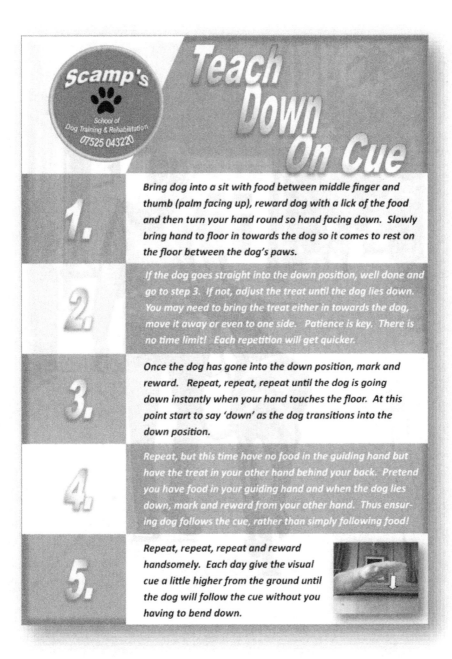

Scamp's
School of
Dog Training & Rehabilitation
07525 043220

Teach Down On Cue

1. Bring dog into a sit with food between middle finger and thumb (palm facing up), reward dog with a lick of the food and then turn your hand round so hand facing down. Slowly bring hand to floor in towards the dog so it comes to rest on the floor between the dog's paws.

2. If the dog goes straight into the down position, well done and go to step 3. If not, adjust the treat until the dog lies down. You may need to bring the treat either in towards the dog, move it away or even to one side. Patience is key. There is no time limit! Each repetition will get quicker.

3. Once the dog has gone into the down position, mark and reward. Repeat, repeat, repeat until the dog is going down instantly when your hand touches the floor. At this point start to say 'down' as the dog transitions into the down position.

4. Repeat, but this time have no food in the guiding hand but have the treat in your other hand behind your back. Pretend you have food in your guiding hand and when the dog lies down, mark and reward from your other hand. Thus ensuring dog follows the cue, rather than simply following food!

5. Repeat, repeat, repeat and reward handsomely. Each day give the visual cue a little higher from the ground until the dog will follow the cue without you having to bend down.

A Good 'Stand' will

'Stand You in Good Stead!'

How Do I Teach My Dog To Stand

To have your dog stand on cue is a useful tool to have in your locker in many situations. One such example is when you want to inspect the underside of your dog or even if you just want to wipe his mucky feet and all he wants to do is lie down, not to mention at the vets or the dog groomers!

It is also the basis of many impulse control exercises and alongside other positional stances, allows us to train focus.

Repetition

Have your dog sit in front of you, take a treat and place it in front of your dog's nose but do not allow him to take it. Slowly move the treat away from the dog, towards your side, parallel to the floor. Simply guide the dog towards you, which means he will have to transfer into the stand position to get the food. If the dog moves back away from the treat, put it back to his nose. If you cannot get the dog to follow a small treat, put a lot of treats in your hand and a small piece between your finger and thumb. This will increase the size of the smell and hence, the temptation of the lure, but only feed the small bit between your finger and thumb when the stand is achieved.

- If the dog's backside keeps going down to the floor, your hand is too high.
- If the dog keeps going into the down position, your hand is too low.

It may be a little tricky at first, but once you have achieved the stand a couple of times the dog will understand this is the stance that he must achieve to obtain the reward   The instant he is standing, release the treat into his mouth. Put your dog back into a sit and repeat the process.

The aim is to have the dog move into the stand position with the back paws not moving at all. In other words, the dog moves his back end up without taking a step.

Once your dog is achieving the 'sit to stand' transfer, place your dog into a 'down' and try having him stand from that position. Exactly the same as the 'sit to stand', except you need to bring the treat up at about 45 degrees.

Again, we are looking at the dog moving to the stand with those back paws nailed to the floor (Metaphorically speaking, of course).

As you are repeating the process you can alternate between sitting and lying down, thus teaching the dog not only to stand from both positions but preventing him from pre-empting what you want from him. This will keep him concentrating on you and not just going through the motions.

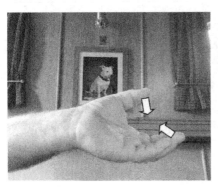 

The visual cue for 'stand'.

Association

As soon as the dog starts to associate getting up from either the sit or the down position for a treat, continue the repetition stage, except now add the verbal 'stand' cue. He will soon start to associate the verbal cue with the motion and will before long execute a sit, down and stand as well as transferring from one to another seamlessly when you request it.

Also, do not forget to swap over to treating from the opposite hand to the one that you are guiding the dog with, so the dog does not learn to simply follow the food.

Ensure that you use the correct visual cue.

Progression

Progress the sit, down and stand at the same time by asking your dog to go from one stance to another and rewarding after completing each task. As he improves, you can treat him for every other action and so on. You can also progress the 'stand' by increasing the gap from the dog moving up into a stand and you releasing the treat, teaching him that a stand command doesn't mean get up on all fours and then do what he likes, it does mean stand up and stay in that position.

What Could Possibly Go Wrong?

Assuming that you move the treat slowly, luring the dog into the correct position, very little. Occasionally, if you don't lift the treat up at the correct angle whilst the dog is in the down position, he may well crawl forward, rather than move into the stand. Personally, in this case I would keep the treat low, encouraging him to crawl, but instead of adding the cue 'stand' add the cue 'crawl' and hey presto you have just taught your dog the neat trick of crawling on command. As for teaching him the stand, start with him in the sit position and as he starts to associate the verbal cue with the action, return to teaching him from the down position. Alternatively, lift the treat at a steeper angle!

Similarly, when transferring from the sit to the stand, if you do not move the treat parallel to the floor, but lift it as you lure the dog, he will naturally lift his front paws off the ground resulting in a jump and grab movement. If this is the case, do not release the treat but put him back into a sit and start again, except keep the treat lower and slowly guide him into the stand moving the lure slightly downwards if necessary.

Starting with the dog in the sit position and slowly luring the dog into the stand position with the treat close to the dog's nose.

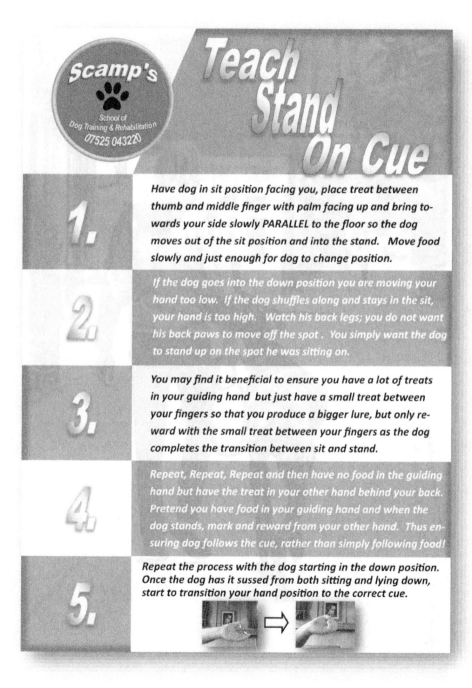

Scamp's
School of
Dog Training & Rehabilitation
07525 043220

Teach Stand On Cue

1. *Have dog in sit position facing you, place treat between thumb and middle finger with palm facing up and bring towards your side slowly PARALLEL to the floor so the dog moves out of the sit position and into the stand. Move food slowly and just enough for dog to change position.*

2. *If the dog goes into the down position you are moving your hand too low. If the dog shuffles along and stays in the sit, your hand is too high. Watch his back legs; you do not want his back paws to move off the spot. You simply want the dog to stand up on the spot he was sitting on.*

3. *You may find it beneficial to ensure you have a lot of treats in your guiding hand but just have a small treat between your fingers so that you produce a bigger lure, but only reward with the small treat between your fingers as the dog completes the transition between sit and stand.*

4. *Repeat, Repeat, Repeat and then have no food in the guiding hand but have the treat in your other hand behind your back. Pretend you have food in your guiding hand and when the dog stands, mark and reward from your other hand. Thus ensuring dog follows the cue, rather than simply following food!*

5. *Repeat the process with the dog starting in the down position. Once the dog has it sussed from both sitting and lying down, start to transition your hand position to the correct cue.*

If you love something, let it go.

If it returns, it's yours;

If it doesn't......

Start at a smaller distance from him!

How Do I Teach My Dog To Come Back (Recall)

Teaching your dog a good recall (or to come back on cue) is essential, and surprisingly easy to achieve. So, why is it that our parks are full of dogs who fail to return when called by their harassed handlers? Perhaps that is because teaching a good, solid recall, takes a lot of practice and patience. Whatever the reason, The MOST important factor is to remember....

- *When the dog gets it right, good things happen to him.*
- *When he gets it wrong, we encourage the right behaviour and then good things happen to him!*

In other words, reward him with the best value treat on offer when he does come back, regardless of how long it took to get him back! Please DON'T scold or reprimand him, just show pleasure that he has come back and reward the recall, as any consequence will be associated with the final recall, not the three hour chase before that. If you tell him off, he will only be more reluctant to come back next time.

What not to do:

- As previously mentioned, scolding or punishing a dog for not returning, will simply enforce the notion that bad things happen when the dog comes back and will reduce the frequency of good recalls.
- Do not only call the dog back when you are leaving the park or going home as the dog will soon learn that, 'Fido, come' means end of play and hence, he is less likely to come back to you when called. Instead, whilst out on the walk, call your dog

frequently, reward him with food, a play or a tug of a toy, etc and then send him away to play again.

- Do not only hold the lead up when you are going home. The dog will soon learn that recall without lead is good but recall with lead in hand is bad. Every so often call him back, clip the lead on and reward, take a few steps, reward again and release him back to play. This will get into the dog's head that recall and having his lead attached is a good thing.

Repetition

It is not a bad idea to prepare for this indoors. Quite simply, say, 'come' or 'here', or another cue if you prefer. Personally, I teach all my dogs to recall on both 'come' and a whistle. This can generally be heard over a longer distance than my voice! Then give your dog a reward and repeat this until he is aware that every time he hears the cue, 'come' he will receive a treat. Once he is responding correctly whenever you ask him to come, start doing this from a larger distance. For example, from the opposite end of the room or even from another room in the house.

Tapping your knees to generate excitement generally helps to start him off, as does holding your arms out as if to welcome him and then bringing your hands into your midriff. When he is coming for the treat every time you request it, he is ready for the great outdoors! A long line (otherwise called a training line or puppy recall line) is invaluable if you don't have a fenced off area to train your meandering mutt.

Some people prefer retractable leads to long lines, but I do not like them at all and if I had my way, I would ban them from being sold. I could bore you for hours with tales of the consequences of their usage. These range from broken thumbs to dogs being killed when broken ratchets enabled them to run into the road, to say nothing of the nasty friction burns to the hand or the devastating effect on the dog's confidence. They also have continual tension and so do not mimic the dog free running as a long line does

There are two basic methods of training your dog to come back when outside. One requires a second person to hold your dog, whilst you back away a few feet, after showing but not giving your dog a treat. You then use your chosen command to call your dog in and make yourself as interesting as possible. You can do this by holding your arms out when you call him, drawing them in until your hands are touching just in front of you and at the height of your dog's mouth. Your helper then releases the dog (still holding the end of the long line if you are using one). Your dog will, all being well, run the few feet and, hey presto, you have your first real recall!

Repeat this and then (as per all the previous exercises) call your dog and have the treat appear from behind you when the dog comes to you.

As soon as he gets to you, release the treat onto the floor, give him lots of fuss and praise and repeat it. As you repeat this action, move away a little further. Increase the distance slowly and if he stops responding over a certain distance, don't be afraid to move back so there is a smaller space between you both.

It is imperative that you heavily reward recall, even at the shorter distances, while training to enforce that coming back when called is a positive choice for the dog and then increase the distance and distraction.

It is like climbing a staircase, with the first step teaching the dog recall from a few metres and the final step having your dog come away from any distraction on command.

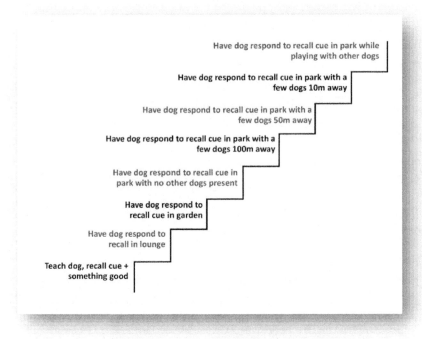

If at any point you cannot get onto the next step, go back down a step and reward more before moving up, or better still, build another step. If your dog recalls when there are dogs 50m away but not 10m away, add that extra step of training when the dogs are 30m away and so on.

Association

Now he is associating the cue for coming back with actually coming back and associating following the cue with receiving a reward, it is time to really drill into the dog that when he comes back good things happen. Reward him every time, even when he has progressed to recalling from large distances ensuring the option of coming back is more rewarding than not. The more we reward this action, the sooner it becomes a learned behaviour.

REMEMBER: When your dog is learning his recall and you are out on walks, once he returns to you it is good practice to clip on his lead, reward him and let him go several times around the walk. This is so he will associate being put back on lead with a reward and not the end of his free play time. Otherwise, he will not be so keen to return the next time you take him out.

Progression

The progression part of the training may seem obvious in the sense that you want your dog to come back from greater and greater distances and this is achieved by building the distance up slowly as mentioned previously, but you also want him to respond quickly and present himself to you in a manner that you can clip on his lead if necessary. The ultimate is a 'round to heel' command (see later chapters), but for now we'll settle for a well-mannered sit.

Initially, lift your hands up slightly as he arrives, just enough for his head to rise and his bottom to lower to the floor as in the 'How Do Teach My Dog to…….Sit' chapter. Once he is sitting (even with a little encouragement) on every recall you can start treating him only when he arrives and sits. It won't be long before the dog is instinctively sitting on his return.

It is a good time to teach your dog to stay while he is learning a solid recall, as both can be progressed concurrently. In the next chapter I will explain how to teach your dog how to stay whilst drilling the recall at the same time.

NOTE: Your dog does not recall consistently because of what you have in your hand, it is because of what appeared from your hands, the many times during training!

Stay Strong

and Teach

your Dog

a Strong Stay!

How Do I Teach My Dog To Stay

In the dark old days when I worked solely with people in factories and not dogs, I spent many years working in what is called Continuous Improvements. This meant I looked at the way companies operated and determined the root causes of inefficiencies or any other issues and implemented better ways of doing things. There was always resistance to change, and the one line that even now grates at me is, 'Well, we have always done it that way, why change now?' Dog training is no different, there are so many things that we used to do that are nothing short of bonkers, that trainers still do because that's what they were shown fifty years ago.

Historically, there were two similar commands used to teach our dogs, 'stay' and 'wait'. I was originally taught that 'stay' was used when we wanted the dog to stay whilst we walked away from him and we expected the dog not to move until we returned. 'Wait' was used when we expected the dog not to move until we called him and then expected him to come to us.

The big issue is this; when you progress the stay and introduce distractions, the dog learns not to move until you return, no matter what. That is fine until you are practising the 'stay' in the park and walk 50 metres away from your dog and then notice that there is a danger behind your dog and so you recall Fido. However, you have taught your dog not to break the stay regardless. Hence, the stay overrules the recall. I *NEVER* want anything to override my dog's recall. On top of that, it is plain bonkers to teach the two commands, when just one serves you better.

It is far more sensible to teach the dog to 'stay' until further instructed, whether that be after I have returned to my dog or called him to me. This method will do just that, as well as strengthening his recall.

Also, if the dog doesn't know whether it is going to be released on your return or asked for a recall, your dog stays focussed, looking for instruction. The key to all good dog training.

Repetition

Start teaching the stay where there are as few distractions as possible, such as a room in your home. Instruct your dog into a sit and put your hand in front of him with your hand flat and fingers pointing upwards (like an Indian 'How' sign).

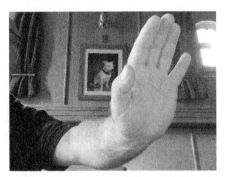

The visual cue for 'stay'.

Don't be lazy at this stage and just point a finger in the air, do use the big flat hand sign. This is what he will see better from a large distance, so you may as well use it from the start or you will have to change it as the dog progresses.

At the same time as making that visual cue, say 'stay'. Keeping one foot where it is, move the other foot back one step and immediately return it back to its original position. Providing the dog has not moved, immediately treat him. It is advisable to keep the treats in your pocket and not in your hand, thereby eliminating the possibility of the dog following the treat in your hand and moving towards it, and you, as you step backwards.

I recommend you take the step back and then forward as quickly as possible, as this will reduce the chance of the dog moving. If he does move, do not treat him, but put him back into the same place he has moved from and repeat the process until he stays for that split second that it takes you to move back and forward again.

When you have achieved this first 'micro' stay, treat the dog then immediately repeat this step again ten to twenty times. Your dog will soon learn that this is the easiest way he has ever earned a reward – just sit there without moving from the spot, and you'll keep feeding him! You can then put him into a sit, show the big hand signal and say 'stay', but this time, take that one step back but then move your other foot back also, then return to your original position and treat him. Now you have, in fact, taken two steps away from the dog. Again, do this relatively quickly. If he moves put him back to his original position WITHOUT FEEDING A TREAT and go back to just one step for a few repetitions. Assuming you have managed the two steps, keep repeating but slow down so there is a second or two after you have stepped back before you return to him. Well done! You are now well on the way to teaching him a good stay.

Association

Now your dog has associated staying where he is with earning an easy treat, it is essential to reinforce both the visual and the verbal signal handsomely. To do this, you make an almost exaggerated signal with your hand as well as a firm verbal 'stay' every time you repeat the process, as well as occasionally just using the visual or just the verbal cue.

This is essential because there will be a time when you are out with your dog and he will be a good distance away and you are far enough away that your voice won't travel. Hence, for his safety, a visual cue is critical (it will also help with his 'emergency stop', see later chapter). Keep repeating, slowly increasing the number of steps you take. If the dog moves, place him back into the position he started from, remembering to withhold any reward. Then simply go back to a few steps less at the next attempt.

Progression

Your dog has now sussed the 'Stay' command, but you need to progress. Your dog will improve quickly if he has sussed that he will be richly rewarded for this, the simplest of tasks.

The key to progression is to keep increasing the number of steps you take before returning to the dog. It is also advisable to alternate between asking the dog to stay and returning to him, and asking him to stay but then altering things by asking him to stay, walking away and then calling him TO you for the treat. Doing this will not only improve the quality of his recall but stop the dog from pre-empting the next move. This will stop him from just going through the motions and will keep his concentration sharper for longer. It also means that when you put him in a stay and then change your mind about returning to him and ask him to come to you, the recall wins and the dog should come running back to you.

It's a good idea to progress the length of time between asking him to stay and you either asking him to come to you or for you to return to his side.   This way we are adding duration to the exercise, not just distance.

To really progress the stay, we need to add distraction, people walking between you and your dog, other dogs in the distance, other dogs close by, noisy children, the skateboard park and so on.   Add the distractions slowly, keeping distance and duration small, then build up slowly, rewarding handsomely.

As he improves at this task, you can then progress the 'stay' even further by asking him to stay and then walking out of sight before returning.   In fact, to obtain many obedience certificates you are required to be out of your dog's sight for a minimum of ten minutes before returning without him moving out of the sit/down position.

What Could Possibly Go Wrong?

Surprisingly for such an important command, there is very little that can go wrong.   Your dog could, however, move too soon.   If this happens, put your dog back into the original 'stay' position.   Now immediately repeat this command but reduce the distance you move away from him, or reduce the time that you are asking him to stay, ensuring he is rewarded handsomely every time he gets it right….and only when he gets it right.

Whether working on a stay or recall, ensure your dog gets plenty of fuss and rewards when completing the action. You can work or shape the quality of the positioning on his return after you have him coming back on cue.

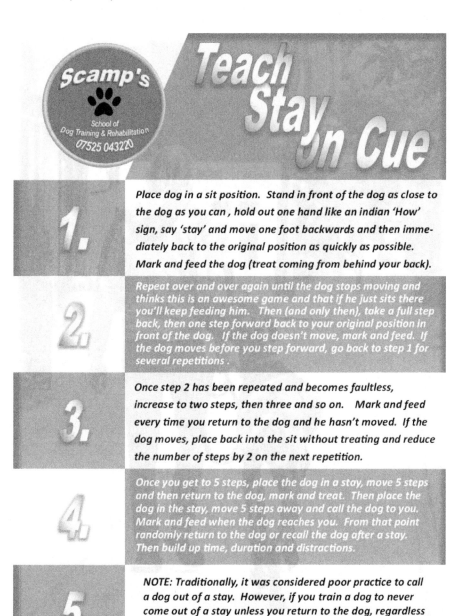

Scamp's School of Dog Training & Rehabilitation 07525 043220

Teach Stay on Cue

1. Place dog in a sit position. Stand in front of the dog as close to the dog as you can, hold out one hand like an indian 'How' sign, say 'stay' and move one foot backwards and then immediately back to the original position as quickly as possible. Mark and feed the dog (treat coming from behind your back).

2. Repeat over and over again until the dog stops moving and thinks this is an awesome game and that if he just sits there you'll keep feeding him. Then (and only then), take a full step back, then one step forward back to your original position in front of the dog. If the dog doesn't move, mark and feed. If the dog moves before you step forward, go back to step 1 for several repetitions.

3. Once step 2 has been repeated and becomes faultless, increase to two steps, then three and so on. Mark and feed every time you return to the dog and he hasn't moved. If the dog moves, place back into the sit without treating and reduce the number of steps by 2 on the next repetition.

4. Once you get to 5 steps, place the dog in a stay, move 5 steps and then return to the dog, mark and treat. Then place the dog in the stay, move 5 steps away and call the dog to you. Mark and feed when the dog reaches you. From that point randomly return to the dog or recall the dog after a stay. Then build up time, duration and distractions.

5. NOTE: Traditionally, it was considered poor practice to call a dog out of a stay. However, if you train a dog to never come out of a stay unless you return to the dog, regardless of distractions, your stay will override your recall, and you NEVER want anything to override your recall.

A Walk in the Park Can be.........

Well,

'A Walk in the Park!'

How Do I Teach My Dog To Walk on a Loose Lead

First of all, if your dog does not already walk on a loose lead, make sure he is wearing a snug fitting 'Y' shaped harness with a front loop.   DO NOT FIX THE LEAD TO THE COLLAR.   If your dog is pulling and the lead is attached to the collar you are risking injuring the dog or restricting his breathing which can cause behavioural or health issues.   The front loop makes teaching a dog to walk on the loose lead much, much easier as this aids turning the dog away from the distraction it is pulling towards without a tug of war.   My personal favourites are the Tellington Ttouch balance harness or the Perfect Fit Harness.   Both are available over the internet.

It is actually really easy to teach a dog to walk on a loose lead, however it does take persistence, patience and a whole load of consistency.

There are many reasons why a dog may pull on their lead. Apart from that in most cases, a dog's natural walking pace is faster than ours, it is worth remembering how dogs learn by association at this point. The chances are that, apart from the vets, every time your dog goes out, it is to go somewhere fun and exciting such as the park or a walk around the block where he can smell lots of exciting scents and he may even get a run or the chance to chase a ball in a large open area. It is not hard to realise why your dog wants to get there quicker, so by walking quicker and being in front of you he will believe he is getting there quicker. If he believes he is getting somewhere quicker by pulling you along then he will consider that pulling as a rewarding behaviour and hence, pulling is a self-rewarding behaviour.

Bearing this in mind, in order to have him walk on a loose lead and stop pulling we need to turn his beliefs on their head and have him believe he will get to his destination quicker if he walks at *your* pace.

There are loads of methods that work effectively, efficiently and ethically and all work on the same principle, but I find the most effective way is to combine two methods. The first teaches the dog to walk on the loose lead but will not stop the dog pulling towards a serious distraction that is higher value than the treats that you are using. The second teaches the dog not to pull towards towards said distractions. I seriously recommend teaching your dog with both methods separately and then combining them for the most effective results.

MOST IMPORTANT OF ALL WE DO NOT USE HARSH PUNISHMENT LIKE YANKING LEADS OR ABUSIVE TOOLS SUCH AS CHOKE CHAINS, HALF CHOKERS, PRONG COLLARS, SLIP LEADS, etc., TO PUNISH THE PULLING. THIS IS UNLIKELY TO TEACH THE DOG TO WALK ON A LOOSE LEAD BUT DOES RUN THE RISK OF DAMAGE TO THE DOG, INCREASING ANXIETY, FRUSTRATION AND REACTIVITY.

As I said, we are going to approach this in a slightly different manner to everything else we have taught the dog to this stage. We are going to do this in two stages and then combine them.   The first stage is to teach the dog to walk nicely by our side and the best way to do this is without the lead and then add the lead afterwards. It may seem long winded but is fool proof and guaranteed.

Stage 1

Start indoors with no lead attached. The easiest way to teach a dog to walk nicely is to start without the lead. Stand still and lure the dog to your side with a treat. Once the dog is standing (or sitting by your side, mark and feed.   Repeat continually, every second, if necessary, until the dog stops moving and just stays by your side. Then start walking but continue to mark and feed every step until the dog is not moving away from you whilst walking and then mark and feed every other step, then every third step and so on. Slowly extend the gap between rewarding until marking and feeding every 10 steps.   If the dog starts to move away, reduce the number of steps between feeding and build up more slowly. Once the dog has mastered walking by your side and being rewarded every ten steps, repeat the whole exercise with the lead attached to the dog but dangling loose. Again, start by feeding every step, then build it up until you are rewarding for the dog walking by your side for 10 steps of a nice walk.

When this is going swimmingly, pick up the other end of the lead and start again.   Once again start off small (feeding every step) and building up to every ten steps.

You now have a dog that is walking on a loose lead. Keep rewarding every ten steps and slowly increase or even 'randomise' the rewarding until you can phase the food out.

HOWEVER, this will teach the dog to walk on a loose lead until there is a distraction worth more than the reward; make no bones about it, your bit of cheese will not compete with a squirrel, a cat or whatever your dog's nemesis is and hence, we have to teach the dog the best way of approaching such a distraction is to walk at Mum/Dad's pace.   So here we go with stage 2:

Stage 2

Forget about rewarding for a moment and we will simply focus on a new method.   We will reintroduce the food in a little while.
We now have two options:

Method 1
Hold the lead by the handle on the opposite side to your dog with your other hand holding loosely on the lead closer towards the dog's collar, ensuring there is sufficient lead between you and the dog in a dip so the lead is effectively creating a 'j' shape. As you start to walk your dog will probably set off and pull straight in front of you. As soon as his head reaches about twelve inches in front of you, walk backwards. Your dog should then turn around and start walking the opposite way.

When his head goes behind you start walking forward again. Once again, your dog should change direction and start walking facing the same direction as yourself. With a little practice and guiding of the dog with your left hand you will be able to get this manoeuvre off to a fine art and ideally your dog will start to turn in an S shape.

Ensure when you walk backwards that you hold your left hand out to your side so the dog can turn and walk between your hand and your hip. Otherwise, the dog will have nowhere to go when you walk backwards and as such will simply walk in front of you.

As your dog starts walking in the same direction as you do again, he will probably, once again, go straight in front of you. You then need to repeat this stepping backwards until the dog's head is behind you, then start moving forward again. This may seem a little fruitless for the first few repetitions but what you are actually doing is starting to teach your dog that pulling actually achieves nothing but to make him turn around in circles. He will soon realise that he will not get to get where he wants to as quickly as if he walked nicely by your side.

You will probably find that the first few repetitions will achieve very little apart from confusing your dog, but when using this method, you will normally see that 'light bulb' moment when the dog suddenly realises that pulling does not pay and resists the temptation to pull in front and walks by your side, if only for a few steps before trying to walk in front of you again. Every time he is turned around he associates walking nicely with reaching his destination more speedily. The more he associates, the more steps he will take by your side, and you will find he will walk on the loose lead, by your side, for a couple of steps, then three or four steps, then five or six steps and so on. The secret is consistency, as it is no good turning your dog around every time he attempts to pull one day, and then changing his associations back by allowing him to pull the next day.

It may mean that when you take your dog out for a walk you may only walk a very short distance due to you having to turn him round every two feet, but you'll find the next day you'll get a little further as the need to having to turn him around lessens, and the next time a little further again. Eventually, you'll find that you are walking without turning him around and hey presto, your dog has learned to walk on a loose lead. After a few weeks, when he is walking well, if he does start to walk a little too far forward a little nudge on the lead will be enough to bring him back to your side as he will be expecting to be turned around and will automatically loosen the lead rather than having to change direction twice.

Method 2

Start with your dog at your side, and a relatively short lead and wait until he is relaxed, then step forward. As your dog pulls in front of you, stop dead and stay stationary. Your dog will probably lean forward on the lead or fidget around trying to get you to allow him to move forward, but with no fuss or communication, stay still until the lead slackens (normally, he'll look up at you as if to ask you why you have stopped). When the lead slackens tell him he is a good boy and step forward again. Keep repeating this process so that every time he pulls in front of you, you stop until you have a loose lead.

He will soon start to associate pulling ahead of you with having to stop and wait. As he makes this association, he will start to walk at the same pace as you do. As with the other methods, there is normally the 'lightbulb' moment when the dog starts to move forward, hesitates and then steps back into line, even if only for one step. If you keep repeating this process, as with the other methods, he will start with one or two steps, then three or four and so on.

With both methods, progression is essential once your dog has taken his first few strides by your side and that is not possible without consistency.

Regardless of which method you have chosen, providing you continue with the process, your dog *will* progress. It doesn't matter whether you are simply stopping when he steps in front of you, turning him round or changing direction, he will spend more and more time walking by your side (to 'heel').

Progression however will be halted when inconsistency creeps in. Remember how I mentioned at the start of this chapter that pulling can be self-rewarding, and so your dog will continue to pull if not taught otherwise. Well, you can spend days walking with your dog stopping or turning and not getting very far but making progress and then you get tired, a little complacency slips in, and you just hold the lead and let him walk with a tight lead (we call this 'dog on a stick'). Your dog has just re-learned that pulling pays and you are back to square one!

To increase the level and the rate of progression you can supercharge the rate of learning by rewarding the dog for being by your side.

Now, you can combine the two stages. Start walking with your dog and if he pulls, walk backwards or stop and when he walks several steps by your side drop him a treat. You will notice he will soon walk on a loose lead beautifully and if he sees something he really wants to get to, whether a squirrel, a tree or another dog, he will look up at you and stay strictly by your side as that is the fastest way to get there.

What Could Possibly Go Wrong?

In a nutshell....lots! However, if you are prepared you can overcome all the potential pitfalls.

If you are using method 1, walking backwards, turning your dog and then moving forward again can be quite tricky at first and the timing has to be good and the motion fluid, or you can end up confusing your dog. Practice will normally sort this out and even a little practising without your dog may be beneficial. If you are still struggling or having trouble walking backwards, simply change method.

When using method 1, if you need to take more than two steps backwards before your dog's head is back in line with your leg then you are more than likely allowing him too much lead.

Another common error is when stepping backwards allowing your arm to move forward resulting in you stepping backwards but the dog stopping where he is, and you end up with the dog ending up further in front of you than when you started stepping backwards. To counteract this simply concentrate on keeping your left hand in line with your waist.

Another difficulty when using method 1 can be turning the dog around. He may not always be as willing as we would like and he will turn a lot easier if, when you step backwards, you move your left hand slightly outwards or inwards, thus guiding him around rather than pulling directly backwards.

The most common fault when teaching your dog to walk nicely on a loose lead is, as previously mentioned, inconsistency. Once you start teaching your dog to walk to heel, never go back to allowing him to pull. It may mean you do not get very far on your first few walks, but the distance walked will soon start to increase. If you allow the dog to go back to pulling, you will undo all the good work that you have already done.

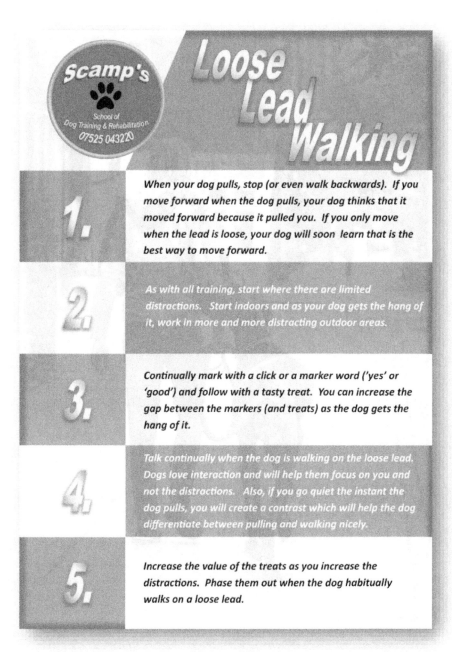

Loose Lead Walking

Scamp's
School of
Dog Training & Rehabilitation
07525 043220

1. When your dog pulls, stop (or even walk backwards). If you move forward when the dog pulls, your dog thinks that it moved forward because it pulled you. If you only move when the lead is loose, your dog will soon learn that is the best way to move forward.

2. As with all training, start where there are limited distractions. Start indoors and as your dog gets the hang of it, work in more and more distracting outdoor areas.

3. Continually mark with a click or a marker word ('yes' or 'good') and follow with a tasty treat. You can increase the gap between the markers (and treats) as the dog gets the hang of it.

4. Talk continually when the dog is walking on the loose lead. Dogs love interaction and will help them focus on you and not the distractions. Also, if you go quiet the instant the dog pulls, you will create a contrast which will help the dog differentiate between pulling and walking nicely.

5. Increase the value of the treats as you increase the distractions. Phase them out when the dog habitually walks on a loose lead.

Good Training..........

Take It or 'Leave' It!

How Do I Teach My Dog To Leave!

'My dog can resist anything except for temptation!'

The 'leave' command is essential for your dog to learn, not only to protect your prized possessions when he mistakes them for his new chew toys, but to ensure that he doesn't hurt himself when he is sniffing a broken bottle he has discovered in the park or about to swallow the potentially fatal slug that he is licking. In fact, it may well even turn out to be the salvation of the neighbour's cat.

Further to that it instils some great impulse control into your dog, teaching him it is a better option to look at Mum or Dad for instruction rather than acting independently, regardless.

In order to teach him to leave on cue you will need two treats, one to tempt him and one to reward him for resisting the temptation.

IMPORTANT *NEVER* allow him to have the 'temptation' treat. In other words, never follow a 'leave' with a 'take it'. Always reward with a different treat to the one you are asking him to leave. The result of rewarding the dog with the same treat that you have asked him to leave is when you see him about to pick up a piece of broken glass, etc. and you request a leave, he will simply wait for the cue to take it and the chances are when you step forward to pick it up, he'll take that as the 'take it' cue and grab it.

'LEAVE' means 'LEAVE', permanently!

Repetition

Start by sitting comfortably on a chair, with your dog sitting in front of you. Hold a 'temptation' treat in a closed fist, so your dog can't get hold of it. Place the closed fist in front of your dog's nose and tell him to 'leave'. He won't, because he doesn't know what leave means and he will try to retrieve the treat. Keep repeating until your dog looks at you for a clue on how to get the food. At this point, as soon as he looks away from your hand, mark or click and simultaneously move the temptation treat away and feed him the 'reward' treat from your other hand. Repeat this over and over again. In a very short space of time, he will look away from the treat in the closed fist as soon as you say leave.

Once you have a successful leave from the closed hand every time that you request it, try with an open hand. When the dog attempts to take the treat, keep your hand where it is and simply close your fist to thwart the dog. (Don't take your hand away). Open your hand and once again tell him to 'leave'. Keep repeating this until you can open the hand say 'leave' and he just looks up at you. Again, at this stage, mark, remove the 'temptation' treat and feed him the 'reward' treat from the other hand. Repeat this until you achieve a 100% success rate.

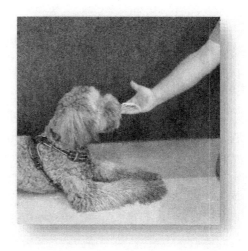

Place a treat on your knee and cover it with your hand. As your dog starts to sniff at your hand and work out how to access the treat, tell your dog to 'leave!'. Unless you are particularly lucky, he will totally ignore you and continue to attempt to relieve you of the treat.

Wait a few seconds and then repeat, keep repeating this until your dog finally realises that he is not going to retrieve the treat and looks up at you for a clue. The second he looks up at you, give him the 'reward' treat (which you will have been holding out of the way in your other hand), pick up the 'temptation' treat and move it out the way.

You've guessed it, repeat continually until he looks up at you for his treat when you instruct him to leave. When he reaches this stage try not covering the 'temptation' treat. Instead, as his nose approaches the treat, adopt a gentle voice and instruct him to leave. If he leaves and looks up at you, you've just taught your dog the leave 'command'.

The more likely scenario is that he'll make a grab for the treat as you lift your hand. If he does, just cover the treat up and, once again, tell him to leave. As before, when he looks up at you, feed him the other treat and move the temptation treat out of sight. Keep repeating this until you no longer have to cover the treat and can simply instruct your dog to leave it.....even if is only for the promise of another reward!

Association

The 'association' stage of this exercise is pretty obvious. The more he starts to associate leaving the treat on cue with the reward when doing so, the more reliable the leave cue will become. It is essential at this stage to ensure that you have a good reward for when he achieves these 'leaves' and it is essential to remove the temptation treat first to prevent him refocusing on it after being rewarded.

Remember what we said at the start of the book, if the dog gets it right, good things happen to him (in this case, he gets rewarded for not taking the temptation treat) and when he gets it wrong, nothing happens (in this case he gets nothing at all for attempting to take the temptation treat).

The more he leaves on command and the more he associates leaving when told with rewards, the quicker it will become a learned behaviour.

Progression

Once your dog is able to leave the treat you have placed upon your knee when asked to 'leave' and can do so without you needing to cover that treat up, the progression is something like this:

- Place the temptation treat on the floor and tell him to leave. If he attempts to take it, cover it up with your hand or foot. If he leaves it, mark it, lift the demonstration treat up off the floor and then feed him the reward treat.

- Leave the treat on the floor for a few seconds before you give him the reward.
- Leaving the treat on the floor, tell him to leave and take a few steps away.
- Leave the treat on the floor, tell him to leave and walk to the other end of the room.
- Leave the treat on the floor, tell him to leave it and walk out of the room.
- Place the treat on his paw and ask him to leave (initially keep your fingers on the treat until he is leaving it)

- Place a treat on the floor outside, tell him to leave.
- Place a toy on the floor, tell him to leave.
- Wait until he attempts to pick up a random item outside, such as a tennis ball, a stick, etc. and tell him to leave it.

Each time he successfully leaves the temptation treat, reward him with another treat, but always remove the original and *NEVER* let him have that one!

What Could Possibly Go Wrong?

Very little, so long as you take small steps and don't rush him. You are expecting way too much if you have taught him to leave a small dog treat at home and then expect him to leave a discarded sandwich in the local park, when he and the sandwich are surrounded by other dogs!

It is quite common for the dog to perfect the leave command indoors and then fail outside. It is always a good idea to keep a ball or a squeaky toy in your pocket and only use this item to reward the very good behaviours. By only using this reward in the case of really good behaviour, you are showing your dog that this is a special treat. This will create an ideal reward to mark his successful outdoor 'leaves'.

When you put a treat on the floor show him the toy, squeak the squeaker, etc., tell him to leave, when he ignores the treat, give him the toy as the reward.

If at any point through the progression, he stops responding to the 'leave' cue, do not be afraid to go back a few steps and build up his compliance again. The leave command is essential and could possibly save his life one day and hence, it is well worth getting right and building it up to a strong learned behaviour.

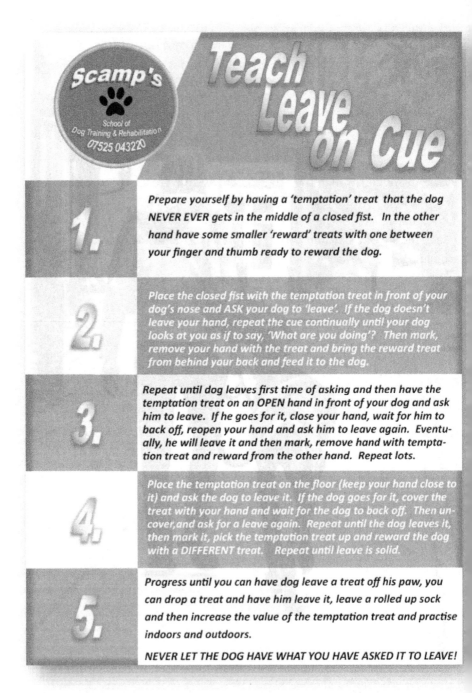

Scamp's
School of
Dog Training & Rehabilitation
07525 043220

Teach Leave on Cue

1. Prepare yourself by having a 'temptation' treat that the dog NEVER EVER gets in the middle of a closed fist. In the other hand have some smaller 'reward' treats with one between your finger and thumb ready to reward the dog.

2. Place the closed fist with the temptation treat in front of your dog's nose and ASK your dog to 'leave'. If the dog doesn't leave your hand, repeat the cue continually until your dog looks at you as if to say, 'What are you doing'? Then mark, remove your hand with the treat and bring the reward treat from behind your back and feed it to the dog.

3. Repeat until dog leaves first time of asking and then have the temptation treat on an OPEN hand in front of your dog and ask him to leave. If he goes for it, close your hand, wait for him to back off, reopen your hand and ask him to leave again. Eventually, he will leave it and then mark, remove hand with temptation treat and reward from the other hand. Repeat lots.

4. Place the temptation treat on the floor (keep your hand close to it) and ask the dog to leave it. If the dog goes for it, cover the treat with your hand and wait for the dog to back off. Then uncover, and ask for a leave again. Repeat until the dog leaves it, then mark it, pick the temptation treat up and reward the dog with a DIFFERENT treat. Repeat until leave is solid.

5. Progress until you can have dog leave a treat off his paw, you can drop a treat and have him leave it, leave a rolled up sock and then increase the value of the temptation treat and practise indoors and outdoors.

NEVER LET THE DOG HAVE WHAT YOU HAVE ASKED IT TO LEAVE!

In Order to Keep Your Dog Safe............

You Need to Pull Out All the Stops!

How Do I Teach My Dog An Emergency Stop

Although the 'down' cue can be progressed into an 'emergency down', a specific stop command is always useful. Your dog could easily find himself in a situation when continuing to do what he is doing would result in him endangering himself or others. It is a relatively easy command to teach and one your dog will pick up quite quickly.

There is a growing number of dog trainers who believe that we should exchange the word 'command' for 'cue'. They feel that "command" resonates with the barbaric dog training methods of old, where dominance and pack theory provided umbrella terms for tactics now deemed to be a form of bullying which has no place in modern day practice. I do agree that 'cue' is the more appropriate, however, any urgent action such as the 'emergency down', 'leave', or 'stop' simply must be a command. We are not requesting a behaviour but insisting that the dog complies. We are however still only employing kind, reward based methods. To obtain good results, we must always use patience, high value rewards and NEVER resort to punishing or reprimanding the dog.

Repetition

This is a nice, easy method to teach your dog to stop on cue, and one which can be done at home in front of the television.

Start by standing in front of your dog with a handful of treats. Take one treat in your right hand, between your forefinger and thumb and hold it as though about to throw a dart. As your dog looks at you, throw the treat (in a dart throwing motion) past or over the dog's head so that he has to turn away to retrieve his treat.

As he is taking the treat put another between your finger and thumb and repeat the action of throwing it past your dog as soon as he returns back to you, preferably while he is still moving towards you. Repeat this action six or seven times so that he is expecting another treat to come past his head every time he looks back at you. Just as he thinks he has sussed the easiest, most rewarding game he has ever played you are going to change the rules.

As he turns to fetch the last treat, make the same shape with your hand as before but on this occasion, keep your hand empty. This time as he returns to you, pretend to throw the imaginary treat with the same motion as when you did use a real one. From the 'about to throw a dart' shape, open your fingers and position your hand so that it is flat and open, just as a policeman would do when stopping on-coming traffic. In a firm voice, say 'Stop!' Your dog will automatically stop moving as he expects a treat to come past his head. Immediately, mark or click and throw a treat underarm from the other hand.

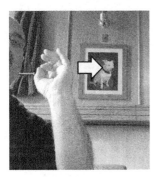 

Repeat the whole process again, throwing treats past him for several repetitions and then have no food, pretend to throw some, changing your handshape from the 'throwing the dart' shape to the stop signal and saying the 'stop' cue. Remember to keep rewarding him for correctly stopping, if only to work out where his treat is.

Association

Your dog will start to associate stopping all motion with the verbal cue in addition to the visual hand signal and this will be reinforced every time you reward him for doing so. After several repetitions of the above process, you should find that you will no longer have to throw treats past the dog before asking him to stop. He will have associated both the visual and the verbal stop cue with being rewarded for stopping. Try this several times a day every day until you have one hundred percent obedience of the 'stop' command and it becomes a learned behaviour.

Progression

The progression stage of this process is essential as it will take him from being commanded to stop as he looks behind for flying treats to halting in full flow as he runs towards you. This is achieved by slowly increasing the distance between you and your dog when you ask him to stop. Once you have reached the point where you can successfully stop the dog from a good couple of metres, it's time to supercharge it by rapidly increasing the distance and start introducing distractions.

When you feel your dog is ready to move on, place him in a sit stay, walk away. When you are a good distance, call him and immediately put up your hand, asking him to stop. The second he stops, mark or click and toss him a good, high value reward. The progression then becomes obvious, increase the distance and then move outside. Keep increasing distance and distractions and if your dog stops responding, simply go back to the point at which he last stopped effectively and start again.

The next progression is having the 'stop' work when the dog is running away from you. This sorts itself as once he learns that stopping on cue pays rewards, he will naturally stop when running away from you and turn around for a treat. The fact he has to turn around will actually make the stop faster, making it more effective than when the dog is running towards you.

You don't have to use edible treats, two balls can be just as effective. Throw one ball for him to retrieve and throw the second as he returns. As he drops the first, pick it up and throw that as he returns with the second. After several repetitions, hide the ball behind you with your left hand and pretend to throw with your right hand, but don't complete the throwing action. Simply move your hand into the 'stop' signal and say, 'Stop'.

As your dog stops and looks up for the ball, mark or click and throw the ball underarm for him with your other hand. This can be slowly progressed to putting your hand up and telling him to stop whilst he is returning to you with his ball in his mouth. As he stops, throw the other ball. Each time you do this increase the time slightly from when he stops to when you throw the ball. This will teach your dog to pause when stopped and give you time to follow up with the next command, as opposed to just stopping at the time of the cue and then continuing in his previous direction.

Once your dog is stopping on cue, it is well worth asking him to sit (or lie down) each time he stops. When you need him to stop in an emergency for real, putting him into a sitting position means it will take him an extra second or so to get back into flight, thus giving you another valuable second to regain control of the situation. That second could well save his life.

What's Your Poison?

Food and Treat Selection

There is good reason why the life expectancy of dogs has been reduced dramatically in recent years. The life expectancy of a golden retriever has reduced by up to seven years. This is understood to be caused by three main factors:

The overuse of unnecessary wormers that destroy the dog's biome (which is the dog's first line of defence against illness). Even the British Veterinary Association now advises vets not to blanket treat parasiticides, although very few vets actually follow the guidelines due to lost trade. Wormers do not prevent the dogs from getting worms, they simply poison and kill any that happen to be in the dog's gut as well as the good bacteria that is essential to the dog's good health. Dogs, contrary to what we are told, rarely pick up worms and you should never introduce a poison into a dog unnecessarily. It is far more sensible to check the dog for worms and then administer the correct (and only the correct) medication when and if required. There are several companies and more and more vets are now offering a 'worm count' service where a simple test of a small sample of the dog's faeces will determine any possibility of a worm. If you are not aware of this service, do have a look at www.wormcount.com. I know many hundreds of dogs that use this service rather than introduce toxins that destroy the dog's natural protection and only one dog that I know of has ever had to require a worming treatment. You wouldn't feed your child aspirin and paracetamol every day just in case he ever gets a headache and neither should we be poisoning our dogs monthly on the off chance they have picked up a worm since the last time we fed them the toxin.

The second reason is the overuse of vaccinations. The original manufacturers of the vaccinations (Pfizer) recommend not to boost any more frequently than every three years. Even World Small Animal Veterinary Association, who advise the national vet associations, advise vets not to give booster vaccinations more frequently than every three years and then not without testing to see if they are required. A simple TITRE test will determine whether the dog's markers are sufficiently low to require boosting. Most vets around the world will refuse to boost any more frequently than three yearly. In fact, due to the possible side effects and the now known longevity of the effectiveness of the antibodies, many states in the USA are refusing to booster any more frequently than every five years.

The other main reason is the increase in branded marketing of diabolical dog food.

The fact that so many bad dog foods that have such a negative impact on our dogs is allowed to be produced and sold in this country is my biggest bugbear (except for trainers that use choke chains and slip leads). Some of the biggest offenders are the large companies with a large advertising budget to match. These brands have become household names and so we naturally assume that these foods must be of a decent quality.

Dogs have a very different digestive system to ours. They do not produce chemicals in their mouth to start processing carbohydrates, nor do they chew their food meaning they slice food into chunks and swallow it in lumps, so they do not get processed until they hit the acid in the stomach. The bowels only have villi to absorb fats and proteins. Ideally a dog should have no more than 3 to 7 percent carbs. The fats (and they must be the right fats and proteins) are the most important factor and then the proteins. They should be getting all their energy from their proteins and fats, not the carbs. When the carbs are too high, the dog stops breaking down the fats, and this will not only negatively affect the whole homeostasis of the dog and will make them prone to weight gain, but to diseases such as pancreatitis. There is only one reason that dog food manufacturers include carbs, grains, rice and other fillers into dog food and that is to bulk it out cheaply and ensure that you have to buy more food in order to keep the dog at a stable weight.

There should be a minimum of 80 percent meat in the ingredients and that meat needs to be of good quality and include several components.

I can almost guarantee that I can tell when a dog is fed a poor food simply by looking at the coat and eyes. It really makes that much difference.

Some of the poorest foods have financial links to the British Veterinary Association, vets, breeders and so on, to create the illusion that they are of a high quality when in fact they will negatively affect the health, behaviour and longevity of the dog. One such dog food which you will see regularly on the shelves of veterinary practices contains up to 97 percent carbs. These foods should go nowhere near a dog far less be promoted at the one place we expect to be advised on the best welfare for our pets.

In most cases there is no such thing as breed specific dog food, so when you look at some of these despicable brands that charge extra for a (for example) French Bulldog, not only is it blatant extortion, but if it is different to that of the standard requirement of a dog, it is by definition, detrimental to the dog. Hence, it is not only not beneficial for the breed but seriously damaging.

Poor dog foods are full of additives, sugars and colourings known to have a damaging effect on behaviour. When I am called out to a dog fed on these brands, I always ask the owners to change over the food and I return in two weeks. I never fail to be amazed by the difference in the dog through simply removing that brand, and the additives loaded into it, from his diet. More than once, I have returned to find resource guarding etc, stopped the day after they stopped feeding these well branded but poor diets.

Other well-known brands can have an adverse effect because they are very sadly lacking in quality ingredients. Dog food manufacturers are not required to list percentage content of their food product, but they do have to list the ingredients in order of percentage of the full content (i.e. whatever is listed at the top of the ingredients has the most content and whatever is at the bottom of the list has the least). Hence, a dog food that has the meat content listed anywhere other than first place is not going to be a quality food.

On top of that you want the meat not only to be specified (i.e. chicken, beef, duck, etc.) but ideally you want to know the cut so you can ensure you are getting the right balance of muscle meat, offal and bone or cartilage.

Avoid ANY food that has ANY of the following words or terms in their ingredients:

- Meat listed as just 'meat'

- Meat listed as meat gravy
- Any meat 'meal'
- Cereal
- Wheat
- Maize
- Oats
- Barley
- Gluten
- Meat and animal derivatives
- Derivatives of vegetable origin
- Sugar in any format
- Salt
- ANY 'E' numbers
- Any description of an ingredient if it is ambiguous. If it is described ambiguously, it is done so for a reason!

That said, there are some excellent foods on the market, but it may take some research, and possibly some trial and error, to discover what suits your pooch the best.

As far as I am concerned the best and most informative website by a country mile (except perhaps mine, he says blatantly plugging his own business) on the world wide web is **www.allaboutdogfood.co.uk** .

It is informative and highly accurate. Please visit it and see how it scores the food you are presently feeding your dog. If it scores less than ninety percent, then you do need to change it over to a higher value food. Find one that scores over ninety percent, and you WILL see a difference in your dog.

Remember that when you change your dog's food, do it over a period of days and as a rule, change the food over as per the following:

Day One	100% old food	0% new food
Day Two	75% old food	25% new food
Day Three	50% old food	50% new food
Day Four	25% old food	75% new food
Day Five	0% old food	100% new food

Hypoallergenic Foods

There are some excellent hydrolysed hypoallergenic foods on the market, however they are particularly hard to get hold of and in most cases completely unnecessary. The mainstream ones are of extremely poor quality and seriously nutritionally lacking. You may well stop the upset tummy, but your dog will be more prone to illness, health issues, behavioural issues, shorter life, etc.

If your dog has an upset stomach, the first step is NOT to source a hypoallergenic food, it is to ensure the food that you are feeding your dog is of a high standard. The biggest cause of colitis in dogs is wheat or gluten intolerance. Most poor foods (including the high-end brands) use wheat to bulk out food and extort you, as the customer, as well as using gluten as a binding agent. In most cases if you change over to a quality food, you will automatically resolve the issue without compromising the dog's welfare.

If the issues persist, then you need to discover the nature of the allergen or intolerance. In which case, transfer the dog over to a single protein food (such as duck or venison) and wait for the tummy to settle down. After a few weeks, add another protein such as chicken, wait a few weeks and add another, etc. When the upset stomach returns you know what the allergen is to avoid. Then pick a quality food (one that scores over 90 percent on www.allaboutdogfood.co.uk) that does not contain that particular allergen.

This process is called 'The Elimination Diet'.

Raw Food (AKA Biologically Approved Raw Food)

Without a shadow of a doubt, the best and most appropriate way to feed a dog is a raw food diet. It is not only biologically appropriate but is what the animal has evolved to gain its nutrition from. Not only does a dog require certain components from its food, but its digestive system also must recognise the form it comes in to break it down and absorb it effectively.

A raw food diet does not mean go and buy some mince from the butchers and feed it to your dog. It must be balanced and complete. This means that we are looking at around a 70:10:10:10 base, which is 70 percent muscle meat, 10 percent cartilage/bone, 10 percent offal and 10 percent fruit, grasses, vegetables, etc. It is also advisable to ensure the food is frozen for a minimum of three weeks before being fed to the dog to ensure any bacteria such as e-coli, salmonella, etc. is not active.

There is a lot of scare mongering (mainly by parties that are funded by poor dried dog food companies) over the safety of feeding raw food, but this is totally unfounded. In fact, the possibility of salmonella is higher in dried kibble than raw feeding, as any bacteria will be inactive due to being frozen and providing the food is thawed out the day before, the possibility of harmful bacteria such as salmonella being present and active is negligible. Dried kibble however, may have all bacteria killed off during the high heat process (that also kills off most of the nutritional qualities), and as such is open to contamination as soon as the packet is opened and as we tend to buy big packs, can be left exposed to the air for weeks or even months.

Raw food should be handled in the same way as any raw meats when cooking, you should always wash your hands after prepping and wash the dish out after feeding, but that is only good housekeeping practice.

There is a huge selection of preprepared frozen raw food available in all pet shops now. The fact there is such a selection with large amounts being stocked in every pet food shop, should tell you there is a seriously large number of dogs fed this way, and there has been no huge reported upturn in salmonella, e-coli or any other bacterial based illness reported by dog owners that would be the case if the risks were as expressed.

There is one downside though. You obviously cannot fill your treat pouch with thawed raw meat to train your dog. With a high quality kibble, you can use all your dog's food for training. With raw you need to reduce the meal size and make up with treats, which is then taking away from the obvious benefit of feeding the most appropriate diet.

If It's Good Enough For Me, It's Good Enough For My Dog…. Or Is It?

Definitely not! By feeding your dog the same food as you eat, you are killing your dog with kindness. A dog has different digestive and nutritional requirements to you and feeding your dog what is suitable for humans has two major drawbacks:

- Some foods that are good for humans are potentially lethal to dogs. (Such as garlic, grapes, chocolate, onions, etc.)
- While your dog is eating human food that he will get no goodness from, he is not eating food composed to give him the essential nutrition needed to live a full and healthy life.

Most people are aware that some foods are unsuitable for dogs, and yet numerous dogs are taken ill even with fatalities occurring over Christmas, simply because dog owners believe they are giving their dog a festive treat. In fact, that bit of mince pie could, and sadly often does, prove to be fatal. Please always remember that a raisin is a shrivelled grape and is therefore highly toxic to dogs.

In addition, feeding your dog with human food can create further problems. If they prefer what you are eating you will probably turn your dog into not only a fussy eater, but one that will probably mither you throughout your dinner!

What are the Best Treats for Training My Dog?

This is a subject that I find particularly interesting. It is important to take into consideration the type of treat that you are using to either lure your dog into a specific action or behaviour, or as a reward for completing it.

Ideally, the treat, whether lure or reward, must be interesting, tempting, tasty, smelly, quick to eat (i.e., not take an age to chew or crunch through and hence slow down the repetition) and yet not filling.

I break any treat I use into small pieces, even small treats will be broken up into pieces. Remember, dogs have a much poorer sense of taste than us (8 times fewer taste buds than we have), and hence, the smell is the rewarding value. You do not want to be replacing their meals with treats, nor do you want to be significantly adding to the dog's calorific intake for obvious reasons.

When training a new dog, I will take training sessions during meal times and use food from the dog's dinner to train the dog. This has two benefits – I am not taking anything away from the dog's nutrition by replacing his planned meals with other treats and also the dog is naturally at his hungriest just before his meal and so will be more responsive to food.

Hierarchy of Treats

An exercise well worth doing with your dog is to choose five treats that you think your dog will respond to, such as warm hot dog, small pieces of cheese, soft pet shop treats, kibble from your dog's dinner and a toy. Have the dog sit in front of you and have one treat in one hand and a different treat in your other hand, slowly move them around the front of your dog's face, allowing him to smell each and then hold them either side of your dog and make a note of which one he takes first. This will tell you which of the two treats are of the higher value to your dog. Repeat this with all the treats and you will soon be able to record a hierarchy of treats (as below) for your own dog. Please bear in mind that it will be different for different dogs.

Scamp

1. *Ball*
2. *Hot Dog*
3. *Cheese*
4. *Commercial dog treat*
5. *Kibble*

Buster

1. *Hot Dog*
2. *Cheese*
3. *Commercial Dog Treat*
4. *Ball*
5. *Kibble*

When teaching your dog to action the 'Leave' command, you would use a low value treat for the temptation treat but give him a high value treat as a reward for leaving it.

When teaching a dog recall, use a high value treat as you are competing with the distractions of the great outdoors like the smell of other dogs' urine, squirrels and the like.

When carrying out basic training such as teaching sit, down, etc., start with a low value treat. As he starts to get bored or less responsive, move on to a higher value treat and he should perk up. Again, as he gets bored of that one move further up the hierarchy. ***Note:*** *Starting* *with the highest value treat means if he gets bored of it, you have nowhere to go!*

How Do I Teach My Dog *Not* To ....

Now this is a whole different ball game, although the same principles apply. Whatever you want to teach your dog *not* to do requires a little thought such as 'What exactly is the behaviour that we don't want our dog to perform?', 'Why is he exhibiting that particular behaviour?' and 'Is there an alternative behaviour that we can teach him that is incompatible with the unwanted ones?'. Once we can answer these questions we can then, knowing what we know from our training principles, start to alter or remove that particular behaviourial trait from our dog.

However, before I explain the above paragraph, I really would like to emphasise that if the issue in question involves aggression, regardless of 'dog to dog' or 'dog to human', please follow the following three points.

- Do not reprimand your dog when he is demonstrating aggressive behaviour as the chances are you will make the situation worse. This is because your dog will rarely associate your reprimand with his behaviour, but more likely associate it with the stimulus (i.e., the dog or person that he is reacting to) and thus escalate the stress and adrenalin levels next time your dog comes across the same stimulus.
- Seek out a dog behaviourist or trainer with experience of dealing with aggressive or reactive dogs. Even if the issue is a relatively small one, it can soon grow out of hand if not dealt with correctly. Ensure the trainer is as good as they say they are – ask for references and make sure they are affiliated to a reputable association such as APDT, IMDT, PPG, ABTC, etc. If you are in any doubt, contact either of the aforementioned associations and ask them to recommend a trainer in your area. Trust me when I say that any cost involved is an investment for the future.
- Do not take the advice of television's 'so called' trainers or a self proclaimed behaviourist who has no formal behavioural education but does have a lot of Tik Tok followers, etc. Ignore

anyone who recommends showing your dog who is boss, executing alpha roles and dominating or bullying your dog. These methods are only televised as they make much more exciting television than the relatively boring spectacle that is effective and ethical training.

How do I teach My Dog *Not* to Jump Up

We ask (or more accurately, answer) the 3 following questions mentioned earlier, as per the example below:

What exactly is the behaviour we want to eradicate?

My dog jumping up at visitors when they enter my house.

Why is he exhibiting that particular behaviour?

He gets excited when we receive visitors, and he is seeking their attention.

Is there an alternative behaviour he can offer that is incompatible with that particular behaviour?

He could meet with all four paws on the floor (he can't be jumping up, if all four paws are firmly planted on the floor).

We can use this information to formulate a plan to change your dog's behaviour in the following way:

Advise visitors before they arrive to have treats ready for rewarding good behaviour (the easiest way is to keep a Tupperware container outside the front door full of treats).

Ask them to turn their back to the dog when he attempts to jump up. We have learned that dogs repeat behaviours when rewarded for them, and if they are seeking attention, any form of attention becomes a reward, including talking to them (even if just to tell them to get off or pushing them down). Hence, we do not want to reward the jumping up, so we ask the visitor not to touch the dog, speak to the dog, not even make eye contact with the dog, but simply turn away every single time the dog jumps up. If the dog repositions himself to the front of the visitor and jumps up again, the visitor must repeat turning away without feeding the dog any attention, until the dog stays calmly on all four paws. This is the point at which the visitor can tell the dog he is a good boy and feed him the treat. If the dog jumps up again, repeat the whole process.

It is advisable to have your visitors drop the treats on the floor rather than put them into the dog's mouth, as once he expects to find the food on the floor, he is more likely to keep all paws planted.

The dog will soon associate keeping all his four paws firmly planted when receiving visitors with a reward and realise that jumping up will achieve nothing.

In the dark old days of training dogs by dominance and using what was called pack theory, basically bullying the dog under the guise of proving that you are the alpha male/female, we would solve this issue by squeezing the dog's paws when he jumped up. The true effect of this is to break down the bond of handler/dog, lose the dog's trust, diminish the dog's thirst for trying new behaviours resulting in making further training more difficult, building up bad associations (with the visitor in this case) possibly leading to aggression, shutting down of the dog and most of all inflicting unnecessary pain on what should be your best friend and companion. Further to this the dog is more likely to associate the pain with visitors arriving rather than his jumping up. The leap to a dog acting aggressively to visitors is then just a short one.

The process of teaching your dog not to jump up may seem all too familiar; if you have worked through the exercises in this book, you would be right to spot the similarities to teaching other commands and behaviours. As explained at the start of this book, the same principles are used in all aspects of animal training – *Repetition, Association and Progression.* Once you start thinking in these terms you can apply these principles to teaching your dog any action, or indeed teach him an alternative behaviour to one that you do not wish your dog to exhibit.

Once the dog stops jumping up, it is critical to continue enforcing the nice greetings with either food on the floor or huge amounts of fuss and attention for many weeks before you phase out the rewards. If you phase out the rewards before it becomes habitual, the dog will simply return to jumping up.

Further Useful Exercises To Teach Your Dog

Your dog now sits and lies down on cue and even comes back when you ask him; why should you teach him anything else? Apart from being good fun, your dog will benefit from mental stimulation as well as physical exercise. I remember the first time I took Scamp (a Patterdale/Staffie cross, who inspired my dog training school) to an agility class. How he slept after I brought him home. He was as fit as you could expect any dog to be and he hadn't run about half as much as he would on one of his twice daily walks, yet he was shattered! It was purely the mental exercise of learning so many new things in one session and, as we all know, a *tired dog is generally a contented dog.*

There is always further improvement and progress to be made to commands that we have already taught our dog. For instance, teaching him 'round to heel'. This is when you teach your dog to approach you from the same side each time he returns to you, walk around your back and end up at the side you walk your dog facing the same way as you are, presenting himself for you to clip his lead on to his collar or harness. Apart from looking impressive, it reduces the time it takes from calling your dog back to moving away from a situation you do not want your dog to be in.

How Do I Teach My Dog To Come Round To Heel

Repetition

First of all, decide the side on which you wish your dog to walk (traditionally the left), then take a treat in the opposite hand and with your dog in front of you, hold the treat up to his nose without allowing him to take it out of your hand. As soon as he takes an interest in it guide your dog around your body with it. When your hand is round your back, in one motion pass it into your other hand and continue to guide him around your back, around to the other side so he is now standing at the side you wish him to walk, facing in the same direction as you. Mark and release the treat into the dog's mouth as the dog completes the motion and stands by your side. Repeat this several times speeding up a little each time.

Association

As your dog begins to associate following your hand around the back of your body until he is standing to heel with being rewarded add the cue 'Round to Heel', and continue repeating. Over a series of repetitions, he will soon learn to walk around your back and present himself for walking to heel with the verbal cue. You will also find it unnecessary to have to move the treat around your back and should be able to slowly transform the action of luring the dog around your back to just holding your hand down by your side and a little flick of your finger towards your back and as he walks behind you and reappears at your other side reward him handsomely.

Once he has the cue sussed, place your dog in a sit or stand/stay, take a few paces back, call him to you and for the first time hold out the treat, guide him around you, saying, 'Round to Heel', as when you first started teaching him the cue. Now, repeat this process, but this time doing just the finger flick and the verbal cue and, with a bit of luck, he will approach you and walk around your back, stopping by the correct side to heel. If he doesn't get it quite right at first, go back a few steps and persevere, he will get there!

Progression

If you consistently ask him to come round to heel every time he comes to you, he will soon do it instinctively as a learned behaviour and, apart from looking impressive, it means every time you call your dog, you will have confidence in the knowledge that you will be able to clip his lead on without having to look where he is, yet alone chase him around to regain control.

Where Do We Go From Here?

The world is your canine oyster

If you have successfully followed the exercises in this book, you will now not only have a dog that will action a number of commands, come back when called, walk on a loose lead, etc., but also have a dog that is keen to learn new tricks, so why stop there? By using the principles in this book you should now be able to adapt these techniques to teach your dog whatever you want. If you want to teach your dog to weave through your legs when you walk, lure him through with a treat, repeat until he associates the weaving with the reward, add a command (such as 'weave'), then progress it until he runs through your legs, whenever you give the cue, impressing everyone at the dog park.

If you are getting frustrated when you need to go out and you let your dog into the garden for his last wee and then you have to wait and wait and wait while your dog walks around the garden sniffing every last blade of grass, then teach your dog to urinate on command. Wait until he is urinating, then say 'wee' and feed him a treat whilst he is mid wee. Repeat this process every time he urinates until he associates the treat with the wee, then progress it by telling him to wee just before he goes and treat him as soon as he starts and you will soon have a dog that urinates on your command, a very useful tool to have in your locker when you are running late for work, etc.

You can always take his training further by taking up any number of activities such as competitive obedience, dog agility, triball, flyball , hoopers, scentwork, rally, canicross, IPO, etc. All of which are excellent sources of both mental and physical exercise and there is no happier dog than a well stimulated, well exercised dog! There are plenty of dog clubs offering all of these activities nationwide and a quick internet search will uncover plenty of options.

So yes, the world is your K9 oyster and there is no reason at all why you can't take your dog's training to the next level and in doing so take your relationship with your dog to the next level too.

Choosing Your Dog

As a Dog Handler Instructor, the majority of my work is rehabilitation based which basically involves dogs demonstrating one or several unwanted behaviours. In most cases there are three reasons for these unwanted behaviours:

- There has been a change to a dog's association to a stimulus (such as another dog has attacked him, making him now stressed at the sight of other dogs).
- The dog has been mishandled (whether intentionally or not) at some point in its life.
- The owner has chosen a dog that is not suitable for their lifestyle/circumstances.
- Poor socialisation or breeding.

The first scenario generally requires professional help from a qualified trainer/behaviourist.

The second scenario is generally the easier issue to resolve as it is mostly a case of educating the owner and a little training.

The third scenario is a lot harder to deal with as if the breed is unsuitable for the owner, there is very little you can do apart from damage limitation or rehome the dog.

It may seem obvious, but there are a lot of factors involved in choosing the right dog for you and your family. You need to choose:

- Breed
- Puppy or older dog
- Rescue/rehomed dog
- Pedigree/cross breed
- Gender
- High energy or one that requires less exercise or stimulation.
- Breed traits

In order to decide on the above, you need to take into consideration:

- How much time can you dedicate to your dog?
- How active are you, now?
- How active will you be in twelve/thirteen years?
- What experience do you have with dogs?
- What do you expect from your dog?
- Where do you live/the home environment?

The above may seem ridiculously obvious, and yet I work with dog charities that take in literally thousands of dogs, because owners thought they wanted a dog for life, but have come to realise that that particular type of dog is not compatible with their lifestyle.

Staffordshire Bull Terriers have been the status dog of the last decade, which has resulted in so many of these delightful, loving pets ending up in shelters, foster homes and unfortunately being euthanised because people have taken one on, purely because it is the fashionable dog to have without researching the breed and discovering they have really low arousal times that can make them appear a little 'full on'. They soon realise there is a lot to owning, exercising and looking after a dog and it doesn't warrant the time or effort to keep such an animal just for status, and the dog becomes just another charity statistic.

All dogs need exercise, some more than others. Collies are working dogs and so require a lot of exercise and stimulation, hence they are probably not the best dog for a couple with limited mobility for example, a husky requires more exercise, has a huge prey drive and is not particularly suited to this country's climate and so is definitely not a suitable pet for mere mortals like most of us that cannot dedicate a large proportion of the day to working with them. They need an owner/handler that can work them for many hours of the day, keep them stimulated, have plenty of training experience and are prepared to work with them almost constantly. Malinois' are super dogs, easy to engage, superbly intelligent, with a great high drive and as such make the ultimate working dog. If you are an experienced dog owner and you want a dog that you will work with several hours per day and wish to compete at IPO or a similar bite work sport, there is no better dog. If you want a general companion dog who you will simply walk around the block a couple of times a day, trust me you are opening yourself up to a whole heap of trouble.

German Shepherds have been selectively bred to guard and react to anything different or suspicious and are as such probably not the best dog to have if you live in a block of flats with thin walls.

Patterdale Terriers are fantastic dogs. I had one that I used as a demonstration/stooge dog. However, they have a high prey drive and are very headstrong making them not the ideal dog for an inexperienced owner/handler.

Due to breeding to specified standards, French Bulldogs and other brachycephalic breeds have inherent breathing issues due to the selfishness of humans breeding for cuteness over welfare and so would not be an ideal companion for a fitness fanatic who wants a dog to take on long runs, three times a day.

There are a lot of older dogs in shelters and rehoming centres that still have plenty of love to offer and would make perfect pets for elderly people looking for companionship. Just as a pedigree puppy would be more suited to a person who is looking for the specific traits of a specific breed.

Mongrels or cross breeds make fantastic pets and generally have better health and live longer due to coming from a wider genetic breeding pool and hence, benefitting from the resilience of several breeds. Rescue dogs sometimes come with a few issues, but with a little patience they can become wonderful pets, giving you the extra bonus of pride in the knowledge that you are responsible for giving this dog a second chance and turning his life around. There are also dogs in rescues because their former owner may have passed away or it has become impractical to care for their dog anymore, and so you could possibly be taking on a dog that is well trained to a good standard, leaving you to develop that according to how you want the dog to continue.

Are you buying a dog just to appease your children and other family members, and if so, are you choosing a dog that will suit them now, or in a few years' time, when they have left home or lost interest, and you will be left caring for the pet?

Will you be breeding the dog? Hopefully if you are reading this section, you are not overly experienced with dogs and would not consider it, but if you are, a family history is essential. As far as I am concerned, the only valid reasons for breeding dogs are impeccable health and temperament alongside improving the lines and breed traits.

NEVER EVEN CONTEMPLATE IT WITH THE THOUGHT OF ANY MONEY THAT MIGHT BE GAINED FROM IT, A RESPONSIBLE BREEDER IS DOING IT FOR IMPROVEMENT AND THE SATISFACTION OF A JOB WELL DONE, NOT PERSONAL GAIN. Only ever contemplate breeding from a dog if you are prepared to do a great deal of research, make sure you have a good match, do a lot of learning and are able to put in a good deal of investment and hard work.

As I work with dog rehoming and fostering charities, I would always ask anyone looking for a new dog to check the local rehoming centres before buying a puppy, but if somebody is set on buying a puppy, then I cannot overly express how important it is to see the pup with its mother in the environment in which it was born and spent its early weeks before you take it home. Ask to arrange to see its father if possible, and if not, the breeder should at the very least be able to show you photos and tell you its full background. Never buy a puppy in a pub or have the breeder bring the puppy to you. There are many dogs being imported from Eastern Europe (see later chapter) that are trapped on the street with high levels of anxiety, pick up lots of bad associations during transportation and are delivered to your house, potentially reactive. It is similar to buying a car off the internet, without looking at it first or test driving it and expecting it to run perfectly.

You wouldn't buy a new car without doing your homework on the type of car that you want or without shopping around, and yet you will probably only keep the car for a couple or three years, so why would you do any different with a pet that will take up a lot more of your time, your life and hopefully stay with you for up to fifteen years?

Your New Puppy

The majority of my work as a dog trainer, involves working with dogs with issues that would have been avoided if the dog had been correctly socialised and trained as a puppy. A responsible and dedicated breeder will have started this process and it is important to continue in as seamless a fashion as you can. I would strongly recommend that you have your new puppy enrolled into a puppy socialisation class as soon as possible. Don't wait until your puppy is old enough to join a class as good classes can sell out weeks in advance. Do your homework - a bad puppy class can do more harm than good. Do not be afraid to ask for the trainer's qualifications and any referrals they may have. A good dog trainer will be only too pleased to show you their qualifications and credentials, as well as any association that they are affiliated to. Ideally, you are looking for a trainer that is a member of the Kennel Club Accredited Instructor scheme (not just KC registered, as that is not policed), The Association of Pet Dog Trainers, the Animal Behaviour and Training Council, the Institute of Modern Dog Training, the Pet Professional Guild or the Pet Professional Network. Do ensure that the trainer displays the Dog Training Charter logo on their website.

This will ensure that the trainer is signed up to a charter stating they will only use kind, proven methods and also, that at some point they have been assessed for their methods and effectiveness. A class that simply allows puppies to play off lead with no structure or recall simply teaches the dog that it is okay to run up to other dogs and become a nuisance when off lead!

'Puppy Parties' are to be avoided at all costs and there is a lot of evidence to suggest that the rise in popularity of such unstructured doggie get-togethers at an early age is partly responsible for the rise in numbers of reactive dogs.

By involving your dog in the early socialisation classes, you will prevent many problems further down the line, for example, poor recall, over excitement when meeting other dogs, aggression, lack of focus, etc.

Outside the class, there is plenty to do that will not only help your puppy understand what is expected of him, but make it a more harmonious and rewarding relationship. The following is a set of guidelines that will help you on your way.

Pet your dog regularly, including holding him, grooming him, touching him all over and rewarding him (giving him little tit bits and treats) for allowing you to do this.

Touch him around his feet, his belly, his eyes, in his ears, in his mouth and around his back end, again rewarding him all the time you are doing this. Not only do this yourself, but rope in other people to do it too. This will ensure no issues in later life when he requires grooming, inspection or treatment at the vets. In the case of male puppies, when they join your family around eight weeks, their testicles will be beginning to show but will not yet be fully descended. Also touch gently around that area and note their progress. Problems are rare, but should anything ever need attention, you will spot it early and the puppy will have no issue with being examined by the vet.

On the subject of vets, every time you pass your vets with your dog, pop in and ask the receptionist to give your puppy a treat. If you don't pass your vets on regular walks, make a trip out on a frequent basis for nothing more than a treat for your new dog. This will build up good associations for the puppy and will be invaluable later in life, when he requires diagnosis or treatment, future jabs and the like.

Another fundamentally important exercise for you and your puppy is for you to feed him a treat and touch his collar as he is taking it. Do this repeatedly and progress this to touching his collar first, followed by a little treat. Then progress to grabbing his collar gently and following with a treat. This will enable your puppy to associate having his collar grabbed and held with good things, which is the total opposite to most dogs that I come across. Generally, dogs will naturally pull away if you move your hand past their eyeline and towards their neck. This can be a serious issue when the scenario arises where you need to grab your dog in a hurry and reconnect his leash. If your dog naturally pulls away, this is practically impossible as he will undoubtedly have better reactions than you.

Training your pup is no different than with older dogs, remember when your pup gets it right, good things happen......but when he gets it wrong the good things don't happen – let him work out that if he does get it right, he will get rewarded. Reprimanding your dog at this early stage can create a lot of issues for him and severely affect your relationship with him. I am not exaggerating when I tell you that the majority of my work involves resolving issues which have escalated simply because his owners/handlers have been repeatedly reprimanding their pet in the belief that they are acting in the poor dog's best interests.

Now for the most important aspect of taking on a new pup; socialisation. This does not mean teaching the dog to play. If you are thinking of getting a new pup, ensure that you read this next section as if you do not socialise your dog sufficiently by the time your dog gets to about sixteen or seventeen weeks, you are seriously risking behavioural issues such as dog or people reactivity.

Socialisation

Did you know your puppy has a natural socialisation period that finishes as early as 16 weeks of age?

This makes it critical that we fully socialise the pup before it gets to that age. If we don't, we are running the risk of owning a fear reactive dog that is likely to act aggressively towards visitors, other dogs, people on bicycles, etc.

What is a socialisation period and why is it so important to get it right first time?

The socialisation period is the time that the pup (or any other animal) would stay right next to its mother's side if left in its natural wild environment. As the mother would never take her young to anything dangerous, the youngster will assume everything that it has been exposed to sufficiently is safe. However, at the age when the pup starts to wander off and see things for the first time by itself, Mother Nature makes a change in the pup to keep it safe. At the age when the pup starts to wander off, it will find anything new suspicious. Take a baby zebra, for example. A mother zebra would never knowingly take her foal to see a lion and so if the change in the brain didn't occur, the first time the baby zebra came across a lion, it would approach it confidently and as such the species wouldn't last too long.

This change happens with puppies as early as sixteen weeks and as such, whatever the pup hasn't been exposed to enough of, will be considered suspicious and that runs the risk of anxiety, which in turn leads to reactivity.

How do we socialise the puppy?

We need to expose the pup to everything that it will meet post socialisation period many times before the period ends. That includes tall people, short people, people of all races, people wearing hi-viz jackets and dogs of all sizes and breeds. We need puppy to be exposed to cats, other animals and indeed any other situation that it is going to experience later in life.

We need to expose the puppy to many, many dozens of dogs in order to ensure puppy will be confident and that causes us a potential issue. We could pick pup up at 8 weeks and then wait for the vaccinations to take effect and so the dog is already 11 weeks before it meets another dog and that only leaves us 5 weeks to socialise the pup. We are already trying to play catchup. We are much better off getting puppy out to see the world from day 1. Carry the dog outside to see other animals and people. Use a dog's buggy to take puppy out (or drive it to the park) and yet still keep it safe while the vaccinations build up puppy's immunity. Take a tarpaulin to the park and place your pup on it, feed him his dinner there and ask passers-by to toss treats for the little one. Let your dog see plenty of dogs and people, even if they are not meeting directly. As soon as the pup is safe on the floor, get him out to meet the world whilst he still considers everything new to him to be safe.

Ask your breeder what they are doing in terms of early socialisation; assuming they are doing their job effectively they will be happy to talk for hours on the measures they are taking to make the puppy's transition as smooth as possible, both to its new home and into the world in general.

Positive Interactions

We need all interactions to be positive. Carry your dog's kibble with you or some high quality treats and have passers-by and visitors to the house feed your dog. Reward your dog for nice positive meets and make it an awesome experience. If your dog is not sure, don't force it. Let your dog take its time if required. Allow it to move away if it desires. If pup raises a paw or sits down and scratches his ear, he is just a little unsure. Give him all the time he needs and if he decides not to meet, allow him not to.

Socialise in ALL Environments

Dogs do not generalise well and so need socialising in all environments. We have a huge amount of *Lockdown Pups* around at the moment that are great with strangers outside, but go to pieces or even attack any visitors in the house because they were brought home during Lockdown and as such didn't see any visitors during the natural socialisation period.

Pup Training and Socialisation Classes

Do book up well in advance for pup training and socialisation classes, but beware, bad classes are worse than no classes. Make sure that the trainers are qualified and affiliated to an association that assesses and polices its members (e.g. APDT, ABTC, KCAI, IMDT, PPG, PPN, etc.) There are still trainers ruining young dogs with electric collars, choke chains, half chokers, slip leads, etc. Don't be afraid to ask a trainer for their qualification and affiliations. Any decent trainer will be only too happy to boast their professional accreditations.

Ensure you see the Dog Training Charter on their website and avoid trainers using terms such as Alpha, Pack, Balanced or use any form of aversive tools such as slip leads, chokers (or half chokers), prong or electric collars.

Seriously avoid any trainer not displaying the Dog Training Charter logo on their website.

Your New UK Rescue Dog

If you have, or you are considering taking on a rescue dog, allow me to take my hat off to you! On behalf of all dogs and dog lovers everywhere, thank you for making this most rewarding of decisions. As much as I take such pleasure in seeing and fussing young puppies out with their new proud families, it breaks my heart every single day to think of the huge number of dogs in rescue shelters and rehoming centres being overlooked while puppy farms prosper and some less scrupulous breeders operate for no other reason than personal gain. Those of you that know me, will be aware that I am a big lump of a bloke that does not suffer fools and can be as hard as nails, yet I do not mind admitting that I have left shelters and rescues in tears. Very often a rescue is a better choice and will become a more reliable loving and faithful companion and enjoy better health than a pedigree puppy. It may even come already toilet trained and with a good standard of obedience and even arrive close to the finished article without you having to do a lot of training or rehabilitation. That said, do be prepared for the fact that any dog that has lived in a rescue environment will need some sort of help to settle in a new home. Be understanding, be patient, and you will be richly rewarded.

Of the many dogs that I have owned and worked with, a cross breed called George who came home with me from Birmingham Dog's Home, not only quickly became the best companion I could ever have asked for but was the dog I have had the least problems or issues with. It was obvious that he'd taken more than the odd beating in his past and was extremely nervous and yet once he learned that he would not get reprimanded for getting something wrong, he would work for nothing more than a little attention or fuss. Because of this, I needed no treats to train him, the reward of a stroke would be enough to ensure he would repeat any wanted behaviour and so he was a breeze to train and recall came naturally to him. He was the envy of all dog owners who knew him and he became my best friend for the next ten years or so that I looked after him before he left this world for the rainbow bridge.

Please do remember that there are considerations that must be made when taking on a rescue dog. There are several reasons why a dog needs a new home, including the following:

- The dog's original owners could have passed away or had to rehome the dog due to their own poor health.
- The original owner did not realise how much work or time was involved in looking after the dog and so gave it up.
- The dog has developed issues or behavioural problems making it impossible to keep, such as aggression towards other dogs or children, etc.
- The dog did not behave in a way the original owner considered acceptable.

The first two would generally result in a perfectly acceptable pet. The other two would probably result in a pet that would require a little work or even constant control and management. It is quite possible that a stimulus has originally created a bad association with the dog and the issue has escalated because of bad handling, or perhaps the issue was originally caused by bad handling, lack of socialisation, training, the dog was taken from his mother too soon, etc. If that is the case, you need to change the bad associations that the dog has, or at least start a basic training programme. Whatever the issue is, the chances are it is reversible and will make owning the dog more rewarding. However, this is not for everybody and it can be expensive employing a professional behaviourist to help you with issue resolution. It is good to gather as much information as you can and if there is none available, ask the staff at the shelter what they have experienced with the dog.

Once you have decided that you want to rescue a dog, what breed or type you want and whether you want a ready-made pet or you are prepared to put some work and time into perfecting a not so perfect dog, speak to the local dog shelters and rehoming centres and let them recommend a dog to you.

Always spend time with the dog away from the kennel before you make a final decision. Most shelters have a room available. You may even be able to look after the pooch for a few nights before taking him on permanently. It is better to meet several dogs and spend time deciding on the right one, than to take on a dog and then find out he is not the one or is not suitable for your lifestyle and then have to re-home him again.

If the dog does have issues and you are not fully confident or experienced, then you will need help from a professional. Often, shelters will have a professional trainer or behaviourist who can help and offer advice. If not, you will need to bear in mind the extra cost involved in employing a trainer over a period of time to change the associations that are creating the issues. DO remember, that the issues could be genetic and so there is always the possibility of owning a dog that needs to be kept away from other dogs, etc. or where you may have to implement some other control and management programme for the life of the dog.

Hopefully, the shelter will have had the dog assessed before they release him for re-homing and that will give you all the information you should need for you to make the decision as to whether that is the dog for you. If the dog has not been assessed, there is no reason why you cannot hire a dog trainer/behaviourist to assess the dog for you. Again, it is better to find out that the dog is not suitable at this stage than after he has settled into what he thinks is his new home.

Rommies and Other Imported Rescues

This is one of the hottest topics in the training world. Ok, let's address the elephant in the room, that no one likes to mention. Most East European imported rescues are street dogs and street dogs are a lot more likely to be reactive, not cope with visitors, be dog and human reactive and resource guard than a well-bred dog from the UK.

Two main caveats here; just because they are more prone to the above does not mean they ALL make bad pets, just they are more likely to suffer from the above. Also, just because they are genetically more likely to be anxious, this does not mean that they cannot have their issues resolved over time with the help of a good behaviourist.

Before any one gets in touch with me to argue that they have a Romanian Rescue and it was perfect, if I cross the road, with my eyes closed, it doesn't mean that I would get run over, it just means that I would be far more likely to get hit by a vehicle. The same with imported street dogs. There is just a much higher risk of anxiety and reactivity.

Although Romanian Rescues make up less than one percent of the population of dogs in this country, they make up over thirty percent of my aggression consults, which gives us an idea of the scale of the issue. This may sound startling, however, when we look a little deeper, it is hardly surprising. There are several reasons why this is the case and in order to understand this, we need to look at how a dog develops in the early stages of its life. The following are the causes of the heightened anxiety in Romanian and other Eastern European imported dogs.

- First of all, if mum is anxious, the cortisol levels (the anxiety or fight/flight hormone) will be high and street dogs are naturally anxious as this keeps them hyper vigilant which in turn keeps them alive on the streets. Anxiety is good for a street dog, just not good for a companion pet. When Mum has high levels the base cortisol level is passed onto puppy and so before the pup is born, it is already prone to anxiety which can develop into fear reactivity.

- Then we have the most important stage of any dog's development, the first five weeks of puppy's life. The more the pup is mothered and licked through this period of the brain development (to be nerdy, the higher ratio of GR and MR receptors in the brain will develop), the more the pup will cope with anxiety triggers without reacting. Obviously, a bitch brought up in this country and bred from, in a comfortable home environment, in a whelping pen with all her needs taken care of by her owner will spend more time licking her young than one that has to source food, shelter and keep a look out for danger. This is because anxiety (or the ability to close down the logical thinking side of the brain and choose fight or flight instantly) is not a good trait in a pet dog as it creates a nervous and reactive dog but is actually what keeps an animal that lives on the street alive.

- The second most important stage of a pet dog's development is the second part of the socialisation stage (8- 16 weeks approx.) This is the stage where any animal still does not leave mum's side in its natural environment and would only be introduced to anything that is good and safe by mum. Once this period ends at around sixteen weeks it coincides with the time when the dog starts to wander off by itself and so has to find anything new suspicious, to stay safe. That is why we take pups from mum at eight weeks old, so that we have a full eight weeks to introduce the pup to anything that it will experience in later life as much as we possibly can in the environment where it will experience them. If the dog does not have enough positive experiences with other dogs in our environment pre sixteen weeks, it will become suspicious of other dogs once it has passed this milestone and as such will remove itself or remove the trigger by using aggressive behaviour. When the dog is on the lead, it has its flight restricted and so will do whatever has the most success in removing the trigger, which is normally lunging and snapping, etc, etc. As the dog has not spent any of its socialisation period in this country and not at all socialised on a lead during this important stage, it is not likely that the dog will cope with the stimuli in our environment without becoming reactive.

- Prior to transportation, the dog is trapped in the street and put into a stressful caged area and so will build up poor associations with people, normally men, that come into its space and as such, alongside not being socialised with people in an indoor setting during its critical socialisation period, is prone to reacting to visitors in the new house.

In a nutshell, imported street dogs have neither the coping mechanisms to deal with anxiety nor did they likely have the correct socialisation during their socialisation period in order to be confident, happy, well-rounded dogs in their new environment. On top of this, food has become a huge resource to a street dog where it is merely a good reward to a specifically bred pet dog that has always been given the correct amount of food and never allowed to starve and so will act differently around food. As I mentioned earlier, all the above increases the probability of anxiety and reactivity in imported street dogs and is not a given. However, as the dogs are ordered, paid for and delivered before you get chance to meet them and have them professionally assessed, you do need to understand the heightened risks before ordering one.

There are genuine rescue centres and associations, that will talk you through the risks and the possibilities that you may have a perfect pet; you may get a dog that requires a lot of time, patience and expensive behavioural assistance or you may have a dog that despite a lot of work will never be comfortable around other dogs, people or visitors to your home. They will explain that you are doing a wonderful service and providing that you are prepared for the potential hard work, time and expense and if you are experienced with working with dogs with potential aggression issues and are happy to take on a possible project dog, then you could not pick a more perfect dog for yourself or your family.

However, there are many misguided but well meaning rescues as well as profiteering companies simply making profit from your kind nature by using emotional blackmail to sell you these dogs without forewarning of the potential issues. They will simply show you a picture of a lovely fluffy dog, tell you it is in a kill shelter and if you do not buy this dog, it will die within the next few days. They will accrue enough orders and send over a van full of bewildered, anxious dogs over the channel and drop one off at your door. We then unrealistically expect these dogs that have evolved to live and survive on their wits in the wild to live harmoniously in our environment.

It may sound like I am down on 'Rommies', but trust me I am not. I love working with these dogs and helping them cope with our world and some do make great pets. I am down on the so-called charities that sell them on to unsuspecting, caring people who are expecting the perfect dog that they were promised, without being advised of the potential risks, pitfalls and without being assured that the new family home is suitable for a dog that has not been bred or socialised for that type of home.

Essential K9 First Aid

In my humble opinion general first aid (for humans) should be taught in every school in the country, just as basic first aid for canines should be part of the testing process for any prospective dog handler when applying for a dog licence. But back in the real world, apart from booking yourself on a canine first aid course, there is very little general knowledge about what to do if your dog requires essential intervention. Hence, I have dedicated this section to the very basics of canine first aid.

The following barely scratches the surface and I would strongly recommend any dog owner to enrol on a one day first aid course. However, for those that do not have the time or inkling I have listed the basics below.

Before we start the basics of canine first aid, we need to define it; First Aid is used with dogs, as with humans, to preserve life and prevent their condition from worsening until those more qualified can take over (with our dogs, this would be the vets).

In order to be prepared, we should carry a canine first aid kit around with us. You can buy such kits, but you would be just as well served to buy a human one and add a spoon, a sachet of vinegar, some bicarbonate of soda (this will become clear later) and lots more various bandages.

Leg Breaks

We could go into great detail about the various bones and types of breaks, but all we really need to be concerned with is whether it is a closed break (i.e. the bone hasn't broken the skin) or an open break (i.e. the bone has broken the skin and therefore visible, and the area around it is bleeding).

Closed Breaks

If the break or suspected break is closed, there is very little to do but get him to the vets as soon as possible. It is essential to get there quickly. The bone may not have broken through the skin and, although there may be no obvious signs of bleeding, you cannot see what is happening under the skin. Dogs have a big advantage over humans with a broken leg, as they have three other legs to balance on. Hence, if they are conscious and moving, simply ensure they have their lead attached and walk them to your car, taxi, vet ambulance, etc. and help them in, taking great care not to touch the bad leg. Trust me, they will keep their leg in the most comfortable position. If you need to pick them up to place them into the transport or if they are unconscious, then lift them from underneath and allow the bad leg to hang free.

Keep them warm whenever possible, cover them with a blanket, your coat or whatever you have handy in case they go into shock.

Open Breaks

Open breaks are a little more involved as there will be bleeding. The bleeding is more dangerous to the dog than the break and so, where possible, you will need to stem the bleeding. Whether you use an item of your clothing or, ideally, a sterile dressing from your first aid kit, you need to cover the area that is bleeding and hold in place with a bandage, or anything else you can improvise with.

Wrap around the wound until all the area is covered, split the end and tie off. **It is well worthwhile to prepare all the bandages in advance. To do this, remove them from their packaging, unwind the first 10 – 15cm and with a sharp pair of scissors cut along the middle of the bandage so as to create two ribbons that can be tied off when applied. Then re-roll the bandage so that the end with the two 'ribbons' is in the middle of the bandage. Once you have done this, wrap in cling film and place in the first aid kit.**

If the blood seeps through the bandage, DO NOT remove it to start again. Simply add another dressing over the top and bandage in place. Be careful not to over tighten the bandage, you are looking to clot the blood, not cut off the supply. Then get him to the vets as soon as possible as per a closed break.

Cuts and Lacerations

You need to stem the blood flow, as with the open break, using a dressing and a bandage. If there is a foreign body such as a piece of glass in the cut, it is imperative that you do not remove it but simply bandage around it. If an object or even his own bone is protruding from the cut, place a rolled-up bandage either side of it and bandage over that. In the absence of spare bandages, rolled up socks work well, if not totally sterile. Again, if blood seeps through, do not remove the blood-soaked bandage, put another one over the top, thus reducing the risk of infection and any clotting that has already started.

A common place for a dog to receive a cut is on the ear. Bleeding from here, as with the tail, can be difficult to stem. If the cut is on the inside of the ear, place the dressing between the ear and his head and strap it in place by wrapping the bandage around the outside of his ear and his head. If the cut is on the outside of his ear, hold the ear flat against his head with the dressing over the cut and wrap the bandage around the ear and his head. In both cases the ear should be strapped flat to the dog's head.

When you are bandaging an ear flat to the dog's head, it is imperative that you use the other ear to ensure the bandage doesn't move. The way to achieve this is to alternatively unroll the bandage in front of the other ear and then behind it and then in front and then behind and so on. If you simply unroll the bandage in front of the non-injured ear when strapping the injured ear flat to the head, your dog will simply pull it off over his face with his paw. If you wrap it just behind the non-injured ear, he will push his head along the floor and hence, the bandage will end up around his neck like a scarf.

As soon as you have stemmed the bleeding, take your dog to the vets- as soon as possible!

I strongly recommend practising bandaging your dog on a regular basis; this will make it a lot easier in a 'real' situation for both you and the dog if practised to perfection.

Shock

If your dog has been involved in an accident, there is a good chance it will go into shock. The visual signs of shock are:

- Rapid weak pulse.

- Increased heart rate.
- Cold feet.
- Possible convulsions.
- Rapid shallow breathing.
- If you press on gums, they stay pale for a long time.

If you suspect your dog has gone into shock you must stem any bleeding, warm him with towels, blankets, etc. (Do not use direct heat) and get him to the vets immediately. It would be advisable to phone ahead so they can be ready for you.

Choking

Choking in dogs is more common than we would like to believe, generally resulting from swallowing balls or parts of broken toys, etc. Another common cause is swallowing parts of rawhide treats. This is not surprising when you consider that rawhide is a by-product of the leather tanning industry and not the pet treat industry. It is made from pressed waste from the leather tanning process, glued into shapes of pig's ears and the like. Apart from the bleaching agents, acid, glue, plastic, etc. that are to be found in raw hide, strips often fall apart inside the dog's mouth as the glue holding it together dissolves when chewed and softened, creating a real choke hazard. As prevention is always better than cure, I would strongly recommend that you reduce the risk to your dog by considering what you give your dog to chew on or play with. Avoiding rawhide, cheap imported toys and balls which fit completely in your dog's mouth is a good start.

However, if the worst happens and your dog is choking, speed is essential. Hence, you need to know the signs of choking and be prepared to act confidently and speedily.

If your dog is choking, the first remedial step is to check if you can see what is blocking his airways and remove it. If you can get the obstruction out, all the better. This can be difficult, so a great tool to keep in your K9 First Aid kit is a metal spoon. Perfect for a swallowed ball! ....and yes, it is possible to damage a dog's throat with a spoon when digging out a ball, but the chances are it will heal. A much happier outcome than you losing your dog through a lack of oxygen.

If you can see but cannot remove the obstruction, then your only option is the K9 equivalent of the Heimlich manoeuvre. Stand behind your dog, place your arms around the dog's belly and link your hands. Then sharply pull up into the dog's stomach four or five times, thus forcing the diaphragm up and, all being well, pushing the air out of your dog's lungs, thus forcing the obstruction up and out of the dog's throat.

Unlike when you carry out the Heimlich manoeuvre on a human, the obstruction tends not to shoot out of the dog's mouth and hence, it will need to be removed from the dog's mouth immediately, before there is any opportunity for him to swallow it again and return the obstructing article to where it was only just dislodged from.

Stings

Again, a common problem which can have serious consequences for your pet. Often, a dog will receive a bee or a wasp sting and will experience little more than some discomfort but, in the worst case scenario, the dog can suffer an allergic reaction which will result in swelling and possible closing of the airways. In this case you need to get your dog to the nearest vet as soon as possible. It is acceptable to administer a portion of 'Piriton' tablet to your dog to stop, or at least reduce, the reaction. Just make sure you phone your vet first to ensure you are giving the right dosage. This will be based on his weight.

In order to take the sting out of the sting (if you'll excuse the pun), you'll need to know whether it was a bee or a wasp sting. This is because one is acidic and the other is alkaline, and therefore you need to treat the sting with something of an opposite pH value to neutralise it. To ascertain whether it was a wasp or a bee, have a look at the area where the dog was stung, he will normally willingly show you the area. If there is still a sting in the area, then it was a bee (and you will normally see the dying bee still on the site of the sting, or nearby where it has fallen). You'll need to remove the sting, being extremely careful not to squeeze the poison sac, which is likely to still be attached (use tweezers if possible). Following this, treat as follows:

- For a bee sting, apply a paste made up of bicarbonate of soda and water. You can simply use a bit of spit to make the paste.
- For a wasp sting, apply vinegar.

My earlier suggestion of adding bicarbonate of soda and a sachet of vinegar to your first aid kit doesn't sound quite so daft now, does it?

Epilogue

There is probably no more varied a career than that of a professional dog trainer. There are days when I get to play with young puppies morning, afternoon and evening, and then there are days when all I seem to do is visit dogs suffering unbelievable anxiety or reactivity. There are days when I feel like I am the luckiest man alive and then there are days when I shed many tears for the dogs that I visit that have suffered in the hands of some unqualified trainer still using tortuous tools to force obedience.

Whereas I fully appreciate that not all issues are caused by poor training, socialisation or nutrition, they do play a huge part and so it is my intention, through my work, my television and radio appearances, seminars and workshops to highlight the importance of kind, ethical, relationship-building treatment of our dogs. Life is so much easier when we get it right from the start and so it is my hope that this book, alongside good training classes (hosted by a qualified and accredited trainer) helps you get the most out of a lifetime with your dog.

I hope that your dog brings you as much happiness as you bring your dog, that your life with your new puppy is all you had hoped for, your new rescue turns out to be your greatest companion, and most of all, I hope that the relationship that you develop with your dog is as rewarding as mine is with my beautiful May.

I wish you and your pet all the very best and hope you have found this book beneficial.

Acknowledgements

Human

My grateful thanks to Emma Partlow, Taylor Richardson and Mike Sher for permitting me to include them in the photographs.

Huge thanks to all my wonderful clients, all of whom have allowed me to make a living working with their amazing dogs.

Canine

Further thanks go to the late Buddy, Buster, Scamp, Logan and George, my companions, my best friends and my inspiration. I think of you all and miss you every single day.